ALISON WESTCOTT

Introducing
Vegetarian Cookery

Illustrated by
GAVIN BINKS

ASHGROVE PRESS, BATH

First published in Great Britain by
ASHGROVE PRESS LIMITED
4 Brassmill Centre, Brassmill Lane,
Bath, Avon, BA1 3JN
and distributed in the USA by
Avery Publishing Group Inc.
120 Old Broadway, Garden City Park,
New York 11040

Originally published as
Basic Vegetarian Cookery

© Alison Westcott 1991

ISBN 1–85398–025–0

Acknowledgements

I still can't believe I've done it! Thanks to Robin Campbell, who asked me in the first place, I've been able to realise my ambition of compiling a cookery book. The interest and encouragement shown by friends and family, especially my mother who has been a great help, have been a tremendous boost. They've also been very willing and much needed guinea pigs, devouring the quantities of food that appeared from the kitchen at various times. It has been an exciting, nerve racking challenge and I am very grateful for the opportunity.

Photoset in Palantino by Ann Buchan (Typesetters)
Shepperton, Middlesex
Printed and bound in Great Britain

Contents

Introduction

This book aims to throw some light on the subject of vegetarian food and the principles involved in this sort of diet. Food bursting with flavour, colour and texture can be made using basic techniques, without fuss, special equipment or skills.

Reasons for trying the vegetarian diet in the first place may vary: increased awareness of health, the wish to avoid meat or just to add a new dimension to your diet. I stopped eating meat whilst at college. If I had been fully aware of the wide scope and benefits of a vegetarian diet then, knowing what I know now, I'm sure my mother would have been a great deal happier!

This book is for people who need to live cheaply and yet also wish to eat nutritious food that is easy to prepare and cook. There are also some interesting facts and recipe ideas for those already aware of what the veggie diet has to offer; and those people who want to try, but do not know where to start, should find some useful information on buying, storing and cooking the ingredients.

I have certainly learned a great deal whilst working on the book. The most important discovery has been 'complete proteins' which is simply what food types are best eaten together to provide the most nutritious meals. Many books do not explain why foods are prepared in such a way, combined with certain ingredients or served with a particular accompaniment. By consulting the simple complete proteins diagrams, you can see at a glance what foods are best used in conjunction with each other.

I am certain you will notice a marked improvement. Eating properly is important, not only for the amount of energy you can muster for your daily existence, but also for your general appearance.

This is a very basic cookery book, so everything has been kept as straightforward as possible. At the same time it attempts to be wide-ranging and provides answers to questions and problems.

Many recipes use similar techniques and most ingredients are found in several recipes, so you can try a variety of dishes without having to buy new ingredients each time. At the end of the day, if I have done anything towards sparking off an interest in the vegetarian way of life, bringing the ingredients off the shelves and into your kitchen, I will be extremely happy.

The Recipes

FOOD FOR VEGANS
(Those who prefer not to eat meat or dairy products)

MARGARINE

Nutter: a mixture of nut oils, which is bought in a pot and is hard. Described as the vegetarian alternative to lard or suet, it can be grated, melted, used in breads and pastry, for example flaky or 'suet' crusts for savoury pies.

Tomor: is the trade name for a margarine especially suited to the vegan diet as it is a pure vegetable product. Many margarines can contain mixtures of animal, vegetable and marine oils and possibly whey. Tomor comes in a block and can be used for cakes and pastries etc.

Granose: is a spreading margarine and contains no animal products. It is low in sodium and is free of lactose.

Vitaquell: is another example of a spreading margarine made from vegetable oils.

SOYA products form an important base for many of the items produced for Vegans as they provide a valuable source of essential nutrients.

Soya Milk: soya 'milk' is a valuable product for vegans – made from soya flour, the milk can be used in the same way as ordinary milk.

Soya Mayonnaise: made by Infinity Foods this is an ideal accompaniment for all cold dishes.

Soya Desserts: a milk pudding made by Provamel in a variety of flavours such as carob.

TVP (Textured Vegetable Protein): this is a processed soya bean product and can be used as an alternative source of protein for vegans and vegetarians alike. It is available in various forms – minced, chunks, 'sausage' mix. TVP has a distinctive flavour and texture that many people find hard to cope with.

Soya Flour: Made from ground dried soya beans, it has a nutty flavour and is a yellowish colour. It is not suitable to use by itself in bread, pastry or cakes, as it has no raising properties, but a few tablespoons can be added to increase the protein content of a particular dish.

Soya Sauce: this is a very well known soya product that is used as a flavouring agent in many chinese style dishes giving a distinctive, delicious flavour. It is an excellent way of introducing protein to vegetable stock, stir-fried vegetables and brown sauces.

Tamari Sauce: a superior soya sauce made in Japan from fermented soya beans and sea salt –it has a rounder fuller flavour. Use as above or add to rice, pulse and nut dishes. Makes a nice addition to salad dressings.

Miso: this is also made from fermented soya beans flavoured with sea salt, sometimes with the addition of whole grains like barley or brown rice. The end result is a thick concentrated paste similar to 'Marmite', which is high in B vitamins and protein.

Tofu: is a soya bean curd almost like junket or yoghurt in appearance. It is made from soya milk. In the West we are just beginning to realise its versatility, and in some of the good health food shops a variety of tofu products can be seen, ranging from the basic blocks of plain tofu to the more exotic smoked tofu, tofu and nut burgers, and delicious tofu spreads flavoured with celery, garlic, herbs or spices.

COCONUT CREAM: a substitute 'cream' can be made by whipping the concentrated coconut block with warm water – an excellent addition for curries or served as an accompaniment to puddings. This product contains no cholesterol.

What is a Vegetarian Diet?

A vegetarian diet is one that is based on the following food groups:
1 DAIRY PRODUCTS
   Milk – whole, skimmed, buttermilk.
   Cheese – hard e.g. Cheddar, soft e.g. Brie, cream, curd, cottage and fromage blanc.
   Yoghurt – low fat, full fat.
   Cream – double, single, clotted, whipping.
   Eggs.
2 NUTS AND SEEDS
   These range from walnuts, almonds, brazils and peanuts to the more expensive cashew and pistachio nuts.
   Probably the best known seeds are sesame, sunflower and poppy.
3 FRUIT AND VEGETABLES
   These speak for themselves.
4 CEREALS AND PULSES
   Cereals include *rice* which can be *long* grain used for savoury dishes or *short* grain for puddings. Cereals also include *grains* such as wheat, oats and barley; these can be used in their whole state or in the form of flours.
   Pulses are the edible seeds of leguminous plants e.g. peas, beans and lentils. Perhaps the best known pulse dish is baked beans although I'm sure it is not thought of in those terms; it consists of Haricot beans.

At first glance, it may look like an unexciting collection of food stuffs. But, when you consider that there are 40–50 varieties of common vegetables, 24 varieties of pulses, over 20 different fruits, 12 different nuts and 9 grains, the picture seems a lot brighter. The potential combinations are inexhaustable. How strange therefore that the majority of people continue with the same old food day in, day out, and stick to the meat and two veg combination.
   It is a fallacy to think that just because there is an absence of meat, the diet will be unbalanced. By that I mean, that the body will not receive the right amount of fat, protein, carbohydrate,

1

vitamins and minerals required for it to function properly. The fact of the matter is, because the diet is more varied, you will have a naturally more balanced food intake without having to try too hard. It is not just the absence of meat that will be of benefit to the body; the very nature of the diet means you will rely on more and more fresh foods, gradually eliminating refined foods altogether.

So many of today's foods are refined beyond recognition. This is a totally unnecessary process which is of benefit only to the manufacturers. In the processing, naturally occurring essential nutrients and qualities are removed, then usually replaced by chemically synthesised versions, but not always in the right proportions. This will upset the balance of the food and could hinder its benefit to the body. It all seems rather a waste of time, so why not eat the real stuff in the first place? Obviously the body will benefit so much more from products in their natural state. But like any diet, it is important to have a good variety of foods to make full use of the range of nutrients that are available and make eating an enjoyable experience.

WHY CHANGE TO A VEGETARIAN DIET?

'We are what we eat'. What a damning but unfortunately true statement that is. It was not long ago that veggie food was synonymous with 'alternative' types who were regarded as rather cranky by the rest of the population. However, the tables have turned and now a larger cross-section of society is taking an interest in the foods and the exciting ingredients included in this sort of diet. It is now becoming a recognised fact that vegetarian food is extremely versatile and satisfying, being full of flavour, texture, and taste, and that what is more, it IS good for you.

There are often articles in newspapers and magazines commenting on the pitfalls of the modern diet. Too much refined food, too much salt, fat, sugar and the increasing consumption of additives, synthetic flavourings and colourings, whilst fresh fruit and vegetables and the all important fibre, are so often lacking in present day eating habits. At first, we tend to brush to one side each new revelation about the damaging effects of our bad eating habits on our health, but, it is true to say that this sort of exposure is having an effect on our eating patterns and very slowly influencing the sort of things that find their way into the weekly shopping basket. As a nation, we are gradually becoming more food conscious, highlighted by extensive media campaigns plainly showing the results of an unhealthy diet which contributes to serious illness, and even premature death. Alarming conditions can be brought on by chemical additives such as, hyperactivity in children, unexplained aggression and in extreme cases, coma. It is therefore understandable that there is a great demand for increased knowledge of just what manufacturers put into processed foods. These days chemical preservatives, flavourings, enhancers and colourings are strictly controlled and have to be clearly shown on the label, so now, at least we have the choice of avoiding them if we wish. Such chemicals are after all potentially harmful and even though research is never-ending in this area, no one can be sure of the long-term effects.

Labelling has been taken a stage further and many articles now show a nutritional break-down giving fat, protein and carbohydrate levels. This information, apart from being interesting, often makes surprising reading: it is quite extraordinary for example just how many processed foods contain large amounts of sugar; this includes sweet and savoury goods.

If you are going to change the sorts of foods you eat, the last thing you will want is to have to traipse all over the town buying a few things here, there and everywhere. Supermarkets do stock basic supplies like wholewheat flours and pastas, the more usual types of pulses and some vegetable oils and margarines. There will of course be the unusual items you will only be able to get from the specialised shop, but, health food shops can be found in most high streets these days. If you are lucky enough to have a 'select yourself' type shop, even better. Here wholefoods can be bought in bulk in plain packets so you can save even more money. As the ingredients are dry, they keep very well when stored in air-tight containers which makes bulk buying extremely good sense both financially and energy-wise. A practical application of the veggie diet is that it really does work out cheaper. No way could you hope to feed four people on eight ounces of meat, but eight ounces of dried pulses can easily do the job for a fraction of the price. You will not need any particular skills to use the ingredients, nor require specialised equipment, however like anything new, it does take a little practice.

Is there life without meat? Well the short answer to that is YES! In the end, it all comes down to a matter of choice. Probably the reason most people change to a vegetarian way of life is because they regard the killing of animals for their meat as unnecessary.

It does seem extraordinary to have to slaughter so many animals when it would be possible to feed more people with vegetable crops for a greater length of time, from the same amount of land given over to the rearing of animals. There is also the bizarre situation in the world where valuable vegetable proteins are grown as fodder crops. These plants in their raw state would provide more food than the final meat product does. Then again, I, like many other people, have discovered that the sort of food in the veggie diet suits them better.

The idea that survival without meat just isn't eating properly is totally misguided, as the section on nutrition will show. The vegetarian diet is a different approach to eating, that is all. It is a collection of tastes, textures and different ingredients combined together in one dish, which is what I like about it. Imagine, bright fresh vegetables, juicy fruit, crunchy nuts, spiced pulses. . . . There is nothing weird and wonderful about these ingredients, granted some of the pulses do have names to conjour up exotic images, try Black-eye peas, Pinto Pigeon peas, Mung and Aduki beans for starters! But what you do with them, that is where the fun starts. You can't make the change soon enough, and you will soon feel the benefits. Experiment with the simple recipes in this book and I'm sure you will be hooked.

AN INTRODUCTION TO WHOLE FOODS

The most fundamental difference between these 'whole' foods and their refined counterparts is the fact that they are WHOLE foods, with nothing added and nothing taken away. The benefits may not seem enormous straight away especially when I say, for example, that brown and white rice contain similar amounts of calories and nutrients, but, the all important difference is, the brown rice has all the natural goodness of the husk, or outer layer, which contributes a valuable source of that vital element roughage, not to mention supplies of vitamins. The advantages must be looked at in the long term. Once you have decided to eat a more natural and healthy diet, your body will respond accordingly, it will not happen overnight, but the foundations will be laid on which to build. Whether it is a case of not feeling quite 'A 1' and not knowing the reason why, or suffering from common ailments such as headaches or indigestion; these are all the body's way of saying that things are not quite right. This can be helped by eating healthier foods, and for those who are overweight, pounds can be lost naturally – now that can't be bad!

The most significant reason for changing to whole foods is the fact that they taste so much nicer and even the smallest amount is enough to satisfy the biggest appetite. You do feel as though you have eaten something, together with the knowledge that it is good for you. How many times have you felt that you could, without difficulty, eat a whole packet of shop-bought biscuits, for example? It would be easy to do, because basically there is nothing to them. One leads to another, then another as the hunger remains unsatisfied. I can assure you, you will not feel the same after a square of Oatcake (see page 149). Here, the ingredients are very much in their unrefined state – jumbo oats, dark brown sugar, treacle and vegetable margarine. At this stage they provide more bulk and so the smallest amount will give the body plenty to work on. Compare this with the highly refined shop-bought biscuits which provide quick bursts of energy, which are quickly used up, resulting in more being eaten to compensate. This in turn means eating very little in the way of goodness and a great deal more in the way of extra unwanted calories. Which is preferable?

Nutrition

If you are able to appreciate how the different foods are made up and how the different elements interact with each other, it will enable you to take full advantage of everything the varieties of foods have to offer.
THE CONSTITUENTS OF FOODS.

Foods are made up of carbohydrates, fats, proteins and a small but vital amount of vitamins and minerals.

1 CARBOHYDRATES

These are required by the body for the production of heat and energy. Carbohydrates are found in natural sugars such as those present in fruit, and in starchy foods e.g. rice, potatoes and grains. Carbohydrates are available in two forms:
a) REFINED: Found in white flour and sugar. Carbohydrates in this form will give quick bursts of energy but they are soon used up and therefore a greater quantity have to be eaten to stop the hungry feeling from returning. Remember what I said about the shop-bought biscuits earlier?
b) UNREFINED: Found in wholewheat flour, brown rice and unrefined sugar. These are the healthiest form as they stay in the body for a greater length of time slowly being broken down and converted into heat and energy.

2 FATS

A layer of fatty deposits protects the nerves, tissues and the organs of the body and helps to maintain the correct body temperature; it carries vitamins around the system and provides an alternative source of energy for the body to draw on.
    Visible fats are found in the diet in the form of butter, vegetable margarines and oils and invisible fats in the form of oil in nuts and seeds.
Fats are used in conjunction with carbohydrates to produce heat and energy and are divided into two categories:

a) POLYUNSATURATED FATS: Found in vegetable margarines like Trex, Nutter, Granose and sunflower margarine and in vegetable oils e.g. sunflower, olive, peanut and corn oils. These are low in cholesterol and are of benefit to the skin, not to mention the heart.

b) SATURATED FATS: These are hard at room temperature and come mostly from animal sources. Consumption of large quantities of this type of fat creates high cholesterol levels in the blood which are linked with heart disease. Therefore the foods to watch if you are a vegetarian are eggs which have a high cholesterol content; closely followed by cheese and butter which are not quite as bad. But before you panic and start thinking about cutting these out of your diet altogether, take heart; beef is 40% cholesterol. It would be easy to eat 8 oz meat in one meal but quite an effort to do the same with eggs or cheese.

3 PROTEINS

These are essential for building and repairing body tissue and are able to satisfy hunger. Proteins are the only food constituent to contain the elements NITROGEN, SULPHUR and PHOPHORUS: these are vital for life as they are used by the body in the construction, growth and repair of the skin, nails, hair, cartilage, tendons, muscles and bones. Proteins help to maintain the metabolic balance by regulating insulin, hormones, antibodies and haemoglobin which is the oxygen carrying pigment in the blood and is itself built by protein. Proteins therefore provide the correct environment in the body for all these processes to continue.

In recent years, research has shown that we require a lower daily protein intake than previously thought. The average man needs as little as 2½–3 oz a day, and only 2–2½ oz is required by the average woman per day. This sort of quantity can be obtained from –
1 pint (575 ml) milk and 2 oz (50g) cheese or
½ pint (275 ml) milk, 1 oz (25g) cheese, 1 medium egg and 3 slices of wholewheat bread.
Put like that, it certainly does not seem very much. To have a similar amount of protein from meat would require about 10 oz (275g) which would make a hefty meal and be very expensive.

PROTEIN FOODS

Milk, eggs, nuts, seeds, cereals and pulses are the sources of protein available to vegetarians. 'Vegetable' proteins, that is, pulses, cereals, nuts and seeds are no longer considered to be second class proteins, (originally, proteins with an animal base were thought to be a superior source and so were called first class proteins) provided they are used in conjunction with other ingredients to make a Complete Protein. This is necessary because vegetable proteins lack one of the essential amino acids.

An everday example of a complete protein would be beans on toast:

Cereals (in this case the bread) are low in an amino acid called Lysine but have high levels of Methionine; pulses (beans) are low in Methionine but have a lot of Lysine. As you can see, if you eat the two together you will make a complete protein.

This idea applies to all groups of foods. Now this does not mean you will have to study in great depth the chemical break-down of each piece of food you eat! The Complete Protein diagrams provide all the information you will need, at a glance, so that each meal you prepare will provide the essential amino acids required by the body for it to function efficiently leaving you feeling satisfied.

As already mentioned, protein foods are made up of amino acids which come in a variety of combinations in the different food groups. Amino acids are themselves divided into two types:

a) ESSENTIAL: These can not be made by the body and so have to be present in the diet in the correct proportion to enable the body to make new protein for use in the system.

b) NON-ESSENTIAL: These are also used for making protein but can be made from other amino acids present in excess amounts in the body.

The quality of the protein therefore depends on its ability to provide these essential amino acids. Providing vegetable proteins are used in the 'complete' way described above, they fulfill all the requirements.

BENEFITS OF PLANTS AS A SOURCE OF PROTEIN

1. All plants eaten as a source of protein such as pulses, contain

the eight essential amino acids when they are combined IN THE SAME MEAL with other protein foods such as rice, eggs or milk. By doing this, they have as much, if not more usable protein than meat.

2. Carbohydrate levels are higher in plants than in meat and as plants are eaten in a whole state, it means more roughage is provided together with protein.

3. Some plant ingredients have the same calorific content as meat; for example, bread, or considerably fewer calories; for example, fruit (⅓ the calories) and vegetables (⅛ the calories).

4. Plant proteins do not contain the potentially harmful saturated fats that are found in animal products.

5. The protein provided by an egg is in an almost ideal form, (in that it provides the correct levels of amino acids needed by the body); this is closely followed by cheese.

6. The protein provided by peanuts is an example of a lower quality protein; that is to say, peanuts lack sufficient quantities of some of the required amino acids. The body can not use low quality proteins as *completely* as the higher ones, so if peanuts are to be included in the diet as a major source of protein, they will either have to be eaten in large quantities, which because of their high calorific value is not such a good idea, or used in conjunction with other protein foods to fulfill the daily protein requirement.

WHY MEAT IS UNNECESSARY

SOYA FLOUR	:	40% usable protein
PARMESAN CHEESE	:	36% usable protein
MEAT	:	20–30% usable protein
PULSES	:	20–25% usable protein
EGGS	:	15% usable protein
MILK	:	5% usable protein

What is all this talk about Usable Proteins I hear you cry! Quite simply, the term refers to the amount of protein eaten, which is in a form readily available to the body. This is linked to what I said about completing proteins. By eating complementary protein foods you will provide the body with nutrients which match its requirements in a form it can use most efficiently. You do not have

to depend on meat as a source of protein; here are the alternatives.
a) Eat larger amounts of the lower quality proteins.
b) Eat alternative animal proteins such as eggs and cheese.
c) Eat a variety of plant proteins, complemented by other foods.
The idea is not to survive on a restricted source of proteins, such as just pulses or rice, otherwise you will be limiting the amount of usable proteins available to the body. The best combination is therefore a mixture of b and c. By taking note of these points and eating a varied diet, any deficiencies in a food will be made up for by another item in the meal.

HOW TO GO ABOUT COMPLEMENTING PROTEINS

We are now aware, (and I can not stress this point enough) that the most beneficial combination is a selection of different plant sources or dairy products together with a plant protein IN THE SAME MEAL. By doing this, the protein content of the meal is increased dramatically. For example, by eating beans on toast (that well known combination) the usable protein is increased three times. Eaten separately, 5 oz of dried beans has 4% usable protein, 1 slice of wholewheat bread has 1.2%, but eaten together they have a value of 15% usable protein. It is such a simple idea, but so clever and not something that is really taken into consideration when planning a meal. This is why I have put together these simple diagrams as a means of quick reference. Now at a glance you will be able to see just what sort of foods you should be eating together, to gain the maximum benefit. Remember, the foods named, serve only as examples.

PROTEIN LEVELS

1. DAIRY – These products have relatively low levels. This is generally the case where the item is consumed in large quantities, for example, milk. 2 cups of milk supply ⅓ of the daily protein allowance. Milk is also a major source of calcium.
2. PULSES – the protein levels found in pulses are equal to if not greater than those found in meat, (especially when com-

plemented). They are in any case the highest plant protein source.

3. NUTS AND SEEDS – These rank behind pulses in the level of protein only because we tend to eat them in smaller quantities as they are sometimes difficult to digest. Three tablespoons of sunflower seeds would supply 11% of the daily allowance, for example, although it might be quite a struggle to eat that amount!

4. GRAINS AND CEREALS – Half the world's protein is provided by grains and cereals. Wheat, rye and oats have 30–35% more protein by weight than rice, corn, barley and millet. DURUM wheat, the type used in pasta is a very high source of protein. A good way of increasing the protein of, for example, rice, is by cooking it with a cereal like wholegrain wheat, or by serving the two together: rice-stuffed peppers with wholegrain wheat salad makes a delicious meal.

5. FRUIT AND VEGETABLES – These contain only small amounts of protein, and therefore should be used in conjunction with other food groups in a meal. Their value lies rather, in supplying large quantities of vitamins, minerals, natural sugars and carbohydrates.

Experiment with milk based sauces; cheese can be added to or used as a decoration on top of dishes, but do not go over-board with the cheese if the dish is a complete protein in itself, but a sprinkling over the top to melt and go brown would certainly not go amiss on some dishes. The same applies to eggs, hard boiled then sliced, crumbled or sieved they are an attractive way of increasing the food value of a meal, as does the addition of chopped nuts, sesame, sunflower or pumpkin seeds; these are wonderful on the top of pies and crumbles as they become toasted during cooking which imparts the most delicious taste and smell.

VITAMINS AND MINERALS

In a well-balanced diet, vitamin and mineral supplements will be unnecessary. Correctly prepared and cooked ingredients will provide all the basic requirements:

a) *Vitamin A*
    Needed for growth and resistance to disease.

Sources: butter, margarine, milk, eggs, carrots, dark leafy
           greens, tomatoes, dried apricots, figs, alfalfa
           sprouts, mangoes, parsley, peppers and watercress.

b) *Vitamin B*
   Composed of thirteen different constituents needed in varying
   proportions, the most important being THIAMINE (B_1)
   RIBOFLAVIN (B_2) NIACIN (B_3) PANTOTHENIC ACID (B_5)
   PYRIDOXINE (B_6) CYNOCOBALAMINED (B_{12}) BIOTIN and
   FOLIC ACIDS (vitamin B complex). These are vital for the
   utilisation of carbohydrates and the functioning of the nervous
   system.
   Thiamine sources: peanuts, brazils, oatmeal, soya flour,
           wheatgerm, wholewheat bread, brewers yeast,
           yeast extract, brown rice, alfalfa, sunflower seeds
           and haricot beans.
   Riboflavin sources: milk, cheese, yoghurt, cottage cheese,
           brewers yeast, yeast extract, almonds, avocados,
           mushrooms and spinach.
   Niacin sources: peanuts, peanut butter, wholewheat bread,
           brewers yeast.
   This gives a rough idea of where these B vitamins can be found.
   As you can see, they are present in very tasty everyday forms.

c) *Vitamin C*
   This is for vitality, building and mending tissues and is found
   in fresh fruit and vegetables.
   Sources: rich supplies are to be found in blackcurrants and
           oranges especially, and also in Brussel Sprouts,
           cabbage, cauliflower, watercress, peppers, potatoes
           and lettuce.

d) *Vitamin D*
   This controls the absorption of calcium and phosphorous,
   which is needed for healthy bones and teeth.
   Sources: eggs, margarine and milk. It is also absorbed by the
           action of sunlight on the skin.

e) *Vitamin E*
   Is needed for fertility and helps prevent premature ageing.
   Sources: vegetable oils, wheatgerm, wholegrains, eggs,

green vegetables, nuts, carrots, apples, muesli and
sunflower seeds.

f) *Vitamin K*
This aids the clotting of the blood.
Sources: soya beans, green vegetables especially spinach,
cauliflower, oats, potatoes, strawberries,
wheatgerm, wholewheat grains.

ESSENTIAL MINERALS

These are found in even smaller amounts in food than vitamins,
but, even so, they are vital for good health. The essential ones are:

a) CALCIUM: sources: almonds, broccoli, molasses, hard
cheese, haricot beans, kelp (seaweed),
milk, sesame seeds, yoghurt.
b) CHLORINE: sources: celery, kelp, lettuce, sea salt, spinach,
tomatoes.
c) COPPER: sources: almonds, bran, brazil nuts, wheatgerm,
wholegrain cereals.
d) IODINE: sources: kelp, sea salt.
e) IRON: sources: molasses, bran, dried apricots, egg yolks,
haricot beans, soya flour, sunflower
seeds, wheatgerm, watercress.
f) MAGNESIUM: sources: almonds, avocados, bananas, barley,
molasses, brazils, haricot beans,
honey, museli, peanuts, wholegrains.
g) PHOSPHORUS: sources: brewers yeast, cheese, eggs, skimmed milk, wheatgerm.
h) POTASSIUM: sources: bananas, butter beans, dried apricots,
figs, haricot beans, jacket potatoes,
lentils, peanuts, soya beans, spinach.
i) ZINC: sources: bran, eggs, nuts, onions, sunflower seeds,
wheatgerm, wholewheat flour.

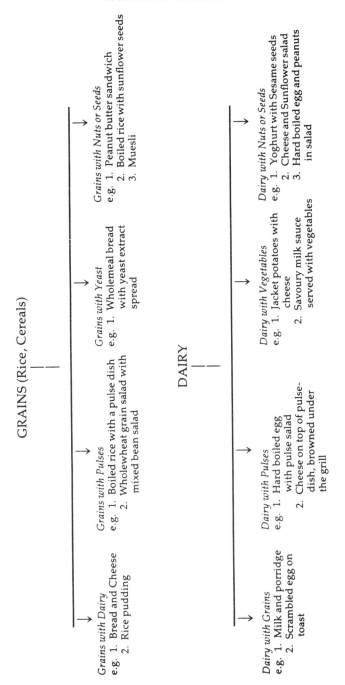

COMPLETE PROTEINS

GRAINS (Rice, Cereals)

Grains with Dairy
e.g. 1. Bread and Cheese
2. Rice pudding

Grains with Pulses
e.g. 1. Boiled rice with a pulse dish
2. Wholewheat grain salad with mixed bean salad

Grains with Yeast
e.g. 1. Wholemeal bread with yeast extract spread

Grains with Nuts or Seeds
e.g. 1. Peanut butter sandwich
2. Boiled rice with sunflower seeds
3. Muesli

DAIRY

Dairy with Grains
e.g. 1. Milk and porridge
2. Scrambled egg on toast

Dairy with Pulses
e.g. 1. Hard boiled egg with pulse salad
2. Cheese on top of pulse-dish, browned under the grill

Dairy with Vegetables
e.g. 1. Jacket potatoes with cheese
2. Savoury milk sauce served with vegetables

Dairy with Nuts or Seeds
e.g. 1. Yoghurt with Sesame seeds
2. Cheese and Sunflower salad
3. Hard boiled egg and peanuts in salad

PULSES (Peas, Beans and Lentils)

Pulses with Grains
e.g. 1. Beans on toast
2. Brown lentil bolognaise sauce with wholewheat pasta

Pulses with Nuts or Seeds
e.g. 1. Lentil patties with peanut butter
2. Chick pea pâté (Hummus) containing tahini (sesame seed purée)

Pulses with Dairy
e.g. 1. Butterbeans in milk based savoury sauce
2. Beans in tomato sauce and omelette

NUTS or SEEDS

Nuts or Seeds with Grains
e.g. 1. Tahini (sesame seed purée) used instead of margarine in a wholewheat sandwich
2. Sunflower seeds with risotto (rice)
3. Walnut biscuits

Nuts or Seeds with Pulses
e.g. 1. Walnut and lentil stuffing
2. Pumpkin seed and bean salad

Nuts or Seeds with Dairy
e.g. 1. Cheese and pumpkin seed salad
2. Milk and peanuts
3. Curd cheese with poppy seeds

Nuts with Seeds
e.g. 1. Peanuts and Sunflower seeds
2. Mixed nut, seed and salad platter

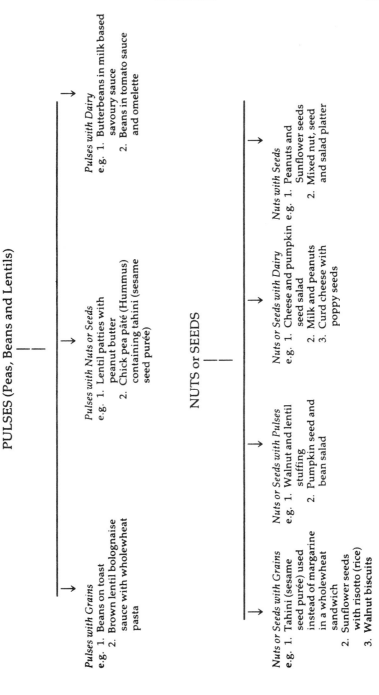

Store Cupboard Ideas

Variety of lentils, peas, beans
Soup Mix (mixture of cereal & pulses, sold in health shops)
Variety of nuts
Seeds – sesame, sunflower, pumpkin
Sultanas
Dried fruit salad
Wholewheat flour:– plain, strong
Whole grain rice
Wholewheat spaghetti, macaroni
Muesli
Jumbo oats
Wholewheat bread
Unrefined sugars
Black treacle (molasses syrup)
Honey
Tinned tomatoes
Tomato purée
Vecon (concentrated veg. stock, sold in cubes/jar)
Dried milk
Carob powder (instead of cocoa)
Peanut butter

Tahini (sesame seed purée)
Chutney
Raw sugar jam
Worcester sauce
Yeast
Yeast extract
Variety of herbs and spices
Sea salt
Black peppercorns
Oil
Wine or cider vinegar
Soya sauce
Cheese
Eggs
Yoghurt
Milk
Butter
Vegetables
Onions
Potatoes
Carrots
Garlic
Fresh fruit

Menu Planning

1. Think of what you will want to cook during the week then shop accordingly, checking the cupboards beforehand. It may sound a bit of a bore, but being organised to a certain extent will save you time through more efficient shopping, preparation and cooking.
2. Be flexible. At the shops you might see things that will spark off ideas. Always buy the best available.
3. Some foods can be cooked for two meals, for example cooking enough butter beans for moussaka one day and butter bean flan the next. Leftover bits and pieces are always useful for risotto.
4. Choose dishes that can be cooked together, either just using the hob or just in the oven – you may as well make full use of the heat.
5. Offer an interesting range of dishes and food during the week, this will prevent 'menu fatigue'. Variety is an important consideration to ensure a wide source of nutrients are made available, then add a splash of colour – a simple sprig of parsley or a slice of orange will do wonders.
6. The vital points of a good meal are; texture, colour, flavour and consistency. Therefore avoid doubling up on these: for example, do not serve a white coloured soup, followed by vegetables in a cheese sauce then a steamed sponge with a sweet white sauce. There is not enough variety of ingredients flavour and colour, texture and consistency are also lacking. Lentil burgers followed by pancakes, for example, may include different ingredients, but they have been cooked in a similar way i.e. shallow fried which means a lot of oil in one meal.
7. There is nothing worse than feeling too full after a meal so plan a light starter to a more substantial main course followed by a light pudding such as fresh fruit or cheese and celery in the case of a three course meal.
8. Make full use of seasonal fruit and vegetables, they will be more reasonably priced and higher in vitamins and minerals especially if eaten raw. Serve a selection of raw crunchy vegetables cut into sticks (crudite) as an accompaniment to a main course, instead of cooking them for a change. It is quicker and healthier.

Pulses

Pulse is the name given to the whole family of dried peas, beans and lentils, which are the edible seeds of leguminous plants. There are many different types, varying in size, colour, and taste and ranging from the tiny green mung bean to the shiny red kidney bean. Therefore, combined with different herbs, spices and vegetables, there is a wide choice of potential pulse meals to explore. Some of the world's greatest dishes are based on pulses. They may not quite have the finesse of haute cuisine, but, when you have a hungry family to feed, they supply a first rate protein.

A quarter to a third of the dried weight (depending on the type of pea or bean) of a pulse is protein. The highest levels can be found in soya: what a cheap source it is too. Cooked with imagination and flair, pulses are truly delicious and provide an excellent way of serving a satisfying meal without making a hole in your purse. They are full of all the nutritional requirements needed by the body when combined with either dairy, grain or seed and nut products. This complete protein seems to happen quite naturally, as for example in, Hummus, the Greek chick pea pâté which contains sesame seed purée (seed) and Indian dhal or lentil purée dishes which are served with rice (grain). Pulses are fairly high in carbohydrates and are not, as most people think, very fattening. They are only about 80 calories per dried ounce which is very reasonable. They only have a trace of fat which is of the polyunsaturated type, so are easily used by the body, and are not stored in the same way as animal fat. They are an important source of B vitamins with notable amounts of minerals like iron, potassium and calcium.

BUYING AND STORAGE

Everyday pulses like lentils, kidney beans, chick peas, green and yellow split peas and butter beans can be found in most supermarkets, but others, such as aduki and mung beans are still confined to the health food shops for a while longer. It is difficult to tell just by looking at the pulse whether it is fresh or old, therefore buy from a shop with an obvious regular turnover of stock.

Once you have bought them, they are very easy to store. Just keep them in air-tight or screw top jars in the cupboard, where they will last for several months without ill effect. But this does not mean they will last indefinitely. Only buy a reasonable amount that you will be able to use fairly quickly, using up each batch before you put the new lot in the jar.

PULSE PREPARATION

1. *Washing and sorting*
   Care needs to be taken especially with the smaller varieties like lentils; they are dried on the ground so foreign bodies, dust, grit, stones and twigs are not uncommon.
   a) The lentils will have to be picked over methodically, moving them in small amounts from one side of a plate to another. This is the quickest way of finding all the unwanted bits. It is well worth taking care; think of your teeth!
   b) Once sorted, put the pulses into a sieve and wash well under the cold tap, moving the contents around to ensure a thorough cleaning.

2. *Soaking*
   Most pulses need to be soaked, as the table will show. This softens the pulse, making it easier to cook and digest.
   a) The long cold soak – pulses are covered in three times their volume of cold water, (i.e. 3 cups of water to one cup of pulses). Soak as the table directs.
   b) The short hot soak – a useful alternative if you find it difficult to plan ahead. Wash the pulses, put in a saucepan with three times the volume of water, cover with a lid and bring to the boil. Boil for three minutes, remove from heat, leave covered for 40–60 minutes. Cook as usual.

3. *Quantity*
   8 ounces (225g) of dried beans or 8–12 ounces of lentils (225g–350g) will be plenty for four people. They may not look like much in their dry state, but remember, they will double in size during soaking.

It is a bore to remember to soak the pulses ahead, but the end result really is worth it. Not only does soaking enable the pulse to soften, but it increases the taste. The pulses do require slightly different treatments, but you will soon get into the swing of thinking ahead. If you cook extra at one time, you will have enough for another meal at a later date. Stored in the fridge, in a sealed container, cooked beans will last for up to five days, they freeze too; this does make all the effort more worth while.

COOKING

1. Always cook the pulses in their soaking water as this is packed with vitamins and minerals. As some of the pulses take up to two hours to cook, the saucepan may need to be topped up to prevent it from boiling dry.
2. Use the cooking liquid in the final dish wherever possible for the same reason, or reserve it and use it for stocks, soups, sauces etc. You may find the liquid from brown or coloured beans a little bitter, so use it sparingly.
3. During cooking a drop or so of oil can be added to enrich the flavour and cut down the amount of foam that appears from the pulses.
4. Always leave the addition of vegetables, herbs and spices until after the pulses are cooked, never salt the water as this prevents them from softening. This does not apply to lentils which benefit from these additions during cooking.
5. Never add bicarbonate of soda during cooking. This does make the cooking quicker but in the process, kills the vitamins and minerals, and often gives a bitter taste.
6. The longer and slower the pulses are allowed to cook the better, as this will enable the full flavour to develop. So, if you have the oven on, they can be cooked at 325°f, 170°c, G.M.3 until tender, or simmer them in a heavy saucepan over a gentle heat.
7. It is very important to remember that kidney beans are brought to a rapid boil for 10 minutes and then left to simmer for at least an hour until they are completely cooked. They can make you very ill if they are not cooked in this way.
8. Split peas and lentils are cooked to a purée. The amount of water or stock used in cooking will affect the end result, so if

you want a stiff purée for burgers for example, use one pint (575 ml) to 8 ounces (225 g) of lentils, and all the liquid should be absorbed.

9. Brown, grey and green lentils do not cook to a purée but they still soften very quickly and should be treated in the same way as the others.

10. Using a pressure cooker if you have one, could be the answer to the lengthy cooking times. At 6.7 kg (15 lbs) pressure, cook pulses for a third of the time shown on the table. Because one batch of pulses will differ from the next, it is best to check before their complete time is up to prevent any chance of overcooking. Some pulses, especially the smaller ones like lentils tend to froth up when they come to the boil. This could block the valve, so add 1–2 tablespoons of oil to the water.

SPROUTING USING A GLASS JAR

Sprouting produces succulent shoots of varying sizes and a whole range of flavours which adds a totally new dimension to salads. It also changes the nutritional structure, by increasing the levels of those vitamins already present and producing vitamin C. It also reduces the amount of carbohydrate in the sprouted pulse, grain or seed.

1. Place 2 tablespoons of the desired pulse in a jar, cover the top with a cheese cloth and cover with a rubber band.
2. Fill the jar with warm water, swill it around, then empty.
3. Cover with warm water again and leave to soak for 24 hours.
4. Drain, rinse again, then pour off the remaining water.
5. Put the jar in brown paper bag, leave in a warm place.
6. The jar will need rinsing and emptying every morning and evening. Sprouting takes about five days depending on the type of pulse. For variations see chart.

HANDY EQUIPMENT FOR COOKING PULSES

The requirements are very simple. A large sieve for washing the pulses; a large bowl for soaking; a heavy saucepan or casserole for cooking, and a liquidiser or food mill for making the purées.

TABLE OF PULSES – 1

TYPE	DESCRIPTION	SOAKING	COOKING	USES	SPROUTING	TASTE/ INFORMATION
ADUKI BEANS	Round, tiny & maroon in colour. They have a sweet flavour, do not overspice	1 hr	30–60 mins	Most often used in one pot dishes, ie. casseroles, stews and risottos. Can be sprouted in salads.	3–5 days	Tastes sweet.
ALFALFA	Tiny seed, nut brown in colour.	None	None	Very nutritious, used in salads.	3–5 days	Juicy.
BLACK-EYED BEANS (or PEAS)	Small, cream kidney-shaped bean with tiny black 'eye' & wrinkled skin.	1 hr	30–60 mins	Used a lot in stews, casseroles. Can be steamed as a vegetable and sprouted for salads.	3–5 days	Savoury, earthy taste sometimes described as musty, therefore goes well with cinnamon. When sprouted they have a strong almost bitter taste.
BLACK BEANS	Long kidney-shaped beans with jet black shiny skins. Not always widely available.	3 hrs	2 hrs	Winter soups, casseroles, complemented by citrus fruits, such as lemons & oranges. Make the most of their luxurious colour.	None	Slightly musty taste with a hint of sweetness.
BUTTER BEANS (LIMA BEANS)	Large, flat and white (or pale green) turning pink or ivory in colour when cooked.	Overnight	3 hrs	Use as for Haricots. Also in casseroles, soup, salads, flans.	None	Strong, savoury flavour, which needs a good strong sauce.

TABLE OF PULSES – 2

TYPE	DESCRIPTION	SOAKING	COOKING	USES	SPROUTING	TASTE/ INFORMATION
CHICK PEAS (GARBANZOS)	Round & creamy in colour, with a slight point at one end.	Overnight	3 hrs. Expand slightly, colour deepens.	Use for spreads such as Hummus, spiced salads & stews, curry accompaniment. Goes well in Mediterranean type dishes.	3–4 days.	Appetising nutty aroma and taste. When sprouted they have a sweet flavour, be careful not to over-sprout.
FENUGREEK	Small brown seed.	None	None	Used as a spice when ground and for salads when sprouted.	3–4 days	Curry flavour which is excellent with egg dishes.
FIELD BEANS	A round-shaped bean with a shiny nut-brown appearance.	2½ hrs	1½ hrs. Have a tendency to split as they get tender.	In casseroles & stews with root vegetables; use beer in the sauce. Good for dishes like Shepherds Pie.	None	Slightly bitter taste (this comes from the skin) so best kept for winter meals.
FLAGEOLET	Slim ovals, pale green or white in colour.	2 hrs	2 hrs	Casseroles or salads. Sprouted – good in salads or stir fried.	3–5 days.	When sprouted they taste like green peas.
HARICOT BEANS (NAVY BEANS)	Small, white and oval in shape.	2 hrs	2 hrs. Expand slightly & turn even whiter.	Salads, casseroles, flans. Sprouted – ideal for Chinese cooking.	3–5 days.	Delicate flavour, do not overdo the herbs & spices. They are firm & crisp when sprouted.

TABLE OF PULSES – 3

TYPE	DESCRIPTION	SOAKING	COOKING	USES	SPROUTING	TASTE/ INFORMATION
RED KIDNEY BEANS	Kidney-shaped with rich red glossy skin	2–3 hrs	2–3 hrs. Swell slightly and turn maroon.	Pâté, spiced or savoury dishes, casseroles, salad.	None	Savoury taste with a floury texture, complimented well by spices & herbs.
BROWN KIDNEY BEANS	Same size & shape as red ones, but are a dull nut colour.	2–3 hrs	2–3 hrs. Swell & go darker brown.	Casseroles, cobblers (scone topped stews), salads.	None	Mealy texture.
RED LENTILS	Either whole or split, they are small & orangey in colour.	None	20–30 mins. Once cooked they go into a purée. Benefit from seasoning during cooking.	Patties, burgers, loaves, stuffing, Dhal, soup, pies. Sprouted – garnish, sandwiches, quiche.	Can only sprout whole lentils 2–5 days.	Always blends well with other tastes & textures. When sprouted they have a good juicy flavour.
BROWN LENTILS (CHINESE LENTILS)	Spherical, small and nut-brown in colour.	None	20–30 mins. Do not readily break up during cooking.	Burgers, stews, excellent with rice, makes a good bolognaise sauce, Lasagne.	2–5 days.	Makes an excellent substitute for minced beef in recipes. When sprouted they have a juicy flavour.
PUY	Tiny & grey in colour.	None	20–30 mins.	Usual pulse dishes.	2–5 days.	When sprouted they have a juicy flavour.

TABLE OF PULSES – 4

TYPE	DESCRIPTION	SOAKING	COOKING	USES	SPROUTING	TASTE/ INFORMATION
GREEN LENTILS (EGYPTIAN LENTILS)	Grey-green colour, slightly bigger than Puy.	None	20–30 mins. Stay whole when cooked.	Usual pulse dishes.	2–5 days.	Peppery flavour especially when sprouted.
MUNG BEANS	Smaller than Aduki. A deep moss green colour.	1 hr	30–45 mins. Retains moss green colour & has creamy texture.	Indian dishes, Chinese style salads.	3–5 days	Savoury flavour. When sprouted they produce the familiar beansprout, which is ideal for salads & stir frying.
WHOLE GREEN PEAS (MARROW PEAS)	Round & apple green in colour.	Overnight.	3 hrs	Soup, as a vegetable.	3–5 days.	Very savoury especially in soup. When sprouted they have a sweet flavour.
SPLIT PEAS (YELLOW or GREEN)	Either yellow or green in colour, medium sized.	None	30–60 mins.	Croquettes, pease pudding, quiche, stuffing, purée, fillings.	Will not sprout.	Green has a lighter taste than yellow. Yellow is slightly 'musty'. Both have a rich flavour.
PINTO PIGEON PEAS	Slightly flattened round, grey with pinkish markings.	2 hrs, swell like raisins.	1½ hrs Dark reddy-brown when cooked.	Casserole type dishes.	None	Bitter sweet taste.

TABLE OF PULSES – 5

TYPE	DESCRIPTION	SOAKING	COOKING	USES	SPROUTING	TASTE/ INFORMATION
SOYA	Round (size of a large pea). Can be yellow, green, brown or black. More usually ivory in colour.	Overnight. Can eat after initial soaking. Elongates to size of peanut, becomes yellow, cream colour.	3 hrs	Common uses. Casseroles & similar dishes. Barbequed beans.	3–5 days.	When soaked they have the taste & texture of green peas. Salt them & use as peanuts. Sprouted: they are the most nutritious of the sprouts, although this is not easy to do.
SPROUTING: OATS	Oval & brown.	None	None	Salads	2–3 days.	Must be hulled, sweet tasting.
PUMPKIN SEEDS	Flat & apple-green in colour.	None	None	Salads & as a garnish	2–4 days.	Unusual nutty taste, use in recipes instead of e.g. peanuts; use as decoration.
SESAME SEEDS	Tiny & fawn in colour.	None	None	Salads & as a garnish	3–4 days.	Must be hulled, sweet tasting. Use sparingly in casseroles etc.
SUNFLOWER SEEDS	Shell has black & white stripes. The hulled seed is light grey.	None	None	Salads & as a garnish	1–2 days.	Hulled ones will sprout, super distinctive flavour.
WHEAT	Oval & nut brown.	None	None	Salads & roast for 20 mins, then add to wholewheat strong flour to make granary flour.	2–4 days.	Rich in B vitamins, sweet taste, good in bread pastry & salads.

Lentil and Lemon Soup with Croutons

1 large onion – peeled, roughly
  chopped
8 oz *(225g)* red lentils – sorted,
  washed
oil
½ teaspoon ground cumin
½ teaspoon ground cloves
2 pts *(1.1 l)* good vegetable stock
2 bay leaves
½ lemon – zest
2 slices wholewheat bread
fresh parsley – chopped

1 Heat a small amount of oil in a saucepan, add the onion, cook until transparent.
2 Add the lentils, cumin and cloves, turn in the oil for a few minutes.
3 Add the vegetable stock, bay leaves and lemon zest, season well with salt and pepper, cover and bring to the boil, reduce the heat and simmer for 35–40 minutes.
4 Just before the soup is ready to be served, toast the bread and cut into small cubes.
Serve the soup warm with the croutons floating on the top sprinkled with the parsley.

Green Pea Soup

6 oz *(175 g)* whole green peas – soaked
  overnight
vegetable stock
1 onion – peeled, roughly chopped
a knob of butter or margarine
salt and freshly ground pepper
bay leaf

1 Soften the onion in a large saucepan with the knob of fat.
2 Drain the soaking liquid off the peas, reserve this and make it up to 2 pints (1.1 l) with vegetable stock.

3 Add the stock, peas and bay leaf to the onion, cover, bring to the boil, then simmer gently for about 2 hours.

Keep an eye on the saucepan; stir occasionally to stop the peas sticking.

The soup will be thick so you can add more liquid if you prefer a thinner one. Season with salt and plenty of pepper. Liquidise if desired.

This has always been my favourite soup. It has a full delicious flavour with great depth, which is surprising when you consider that it is made from such simple ingredients. It will benefit from a really good stock, see page 169.

Quick Kidney Bean and Orange Pâté

8 oz (225 g) cooked kidney beans
1 clove garlic – peeled, crushed
1 dessertspoon white wine vinegar
1 orange – zest and juice
1 teaspoon sage
1 teaspoon mixed herbs
½ teaspoon thyme
salt and freshly ground pepper
1 tablespoon oil

If you have a food processor, put all the ingredients in together and give them a whizz. If not, mash the beans with a fork then add the bits and beat.

It is best left in the fridge for a while to allow the flavours to mingle and develop.

This recipe idea is an easy way of making something quick and tasty with extra pulse you might have cooked during the week, ideal for Saturday lunch time served with hot toast or crackers. The method will be the same whatever pulse is used, so experiment with different herbs and spices.

Hummus (Chick Pea Pâté or Dip)

8 oz *(225 g)* chick peas – washed, soaked overnight
1 clove garlic – peeled, crushed
1 tablespoon oil
3 tablespoons Tahini (sesame seed purée)
2 lemons – zest and juice
salt and freshly ground pepper

decoration:
paprika and snipped parsley

1 Put the chick peas with the soaking water in a saucepan, cover and bring to the boil, reduce the heat and simmer until cooked – approximately 2 hours.
2 When cooked, drain reserving ¼ pint (150 ml) of the liquid.
3 Put the chick peas, cooking liquid, garlic and oil into the food processor or liquidiser, whizz to form a smoothish paste.
If you don't have a liquidiser, rub the mixture through a sieve using the back of a spoon or simply mush with a fork, which will give an attractive coarse texture.
4 Transfer to a bowl, beat in the tahini and lemon zest. Season with some lemon juice, salt and pepper to taste. Leave in the fridge to chill.

To serve, transfer to a clean bowl, sprinkle with a couple of pinches of paprika in the middle and place a bit of snipped parsley on the top.

Eat with fingers of toast, wholewheat pitta bread or sticks of raw vegetables.

Shepherds Pie

Oven: 350°f, 180°c, G.M.4

1 large onion – peeled, roughly
    chopped
oil
12 oz *(350 g)* brown lentils – sorted
    and washed
1 pt *(575 ml)* water
1 good teaspoon Vecon or yeast
    extract
2 tablespoons Worcester sauce
1 good tablespoon Tahini (sesame
    seed purée)
salt and freshly ground pepper

Topping:
1½–2 lbs potatoes – washed
knob of butter
salt and freshly ground pepper
grated nutmeg

1 Soften the onion in a little oil in a saucepan, cover. When it is
   transparent add the lentils. Turn them in the oil to coat well,
   cook for a couple of minutes.

2 Add the water, Vecon (or yeast extract), Worcester sauce, salt
   and pepper. Cover. Simmer gently until the lentils are soft.

3 Add the Tahini, stir well, this will thicken the sauce a little.
   Adjust the seasoning with salt, pepper and more Worcester
   sauce if required. Transfer to an ovenproof dish.
   The dish can be prepared to this stage well in advance if
   necessary.

4 Put the whole washed potatoes into a saucepan of cold salted
   water, cover and bring to the boil, reduce the heat and simmer
   for 20 minutes or until cooked. To test if done, they should easily
   slip off the blade of a knife.

5 Drain the potatoes well. Mash together with the butter, season
   with salt, pepper and freshly grated nutmeg to taste.

6 Spread the potato on the top of the lentil base. Run a fork across
   the top to make a simple decoration.

   Bake in the oven for 30–35 minutes until the top is nicely
   browned.

Kidney Bean Surprise

8 oz *(225 g)* dried kidney beans – washed, soaked
1 large onion – peeled, roughly chopped
1 clove garlic – peeled, crushed
oil
8 oz *(225 g)* mushrooms – wiped, sliced
1 lemon – juice
1 teaspoon ground cumin
½ teaspoon ground ginger
1 teaspoon ground coriander
4 tablespoons natural yoghurt
2 teaspoons tomato purée

freshly chopped parsley to decorate

So called because it was an unexpected surprise that it tasted so good!

1 Put the kidney beans and their soaking water into a saucepan, cover and bring to a rapid boil for 10 minutes. Reduce the heat and simmer gently until tender (approximately 1 hour). Keep an eye on them, the pan might need topping up with water. Drain once cooked.

2 Heat a small amount of oil in a saucepan. Soften the onion and garlic until the onion is transparent.

3 Add the spices, stir well and cook for a further minute.

4 Add the mushrooms, cook slightly.

5 Blend the tomato purée with the yoghurt, add this to the onion mix.

6 Add the drained beans, stir well.

7 Heat through gently. Serve decorated with chopped parsley if desired.

For a complete protein meal serve with a rice or grain dish or add nuts. These can be cooked with the onions in the beginning to increase their flavour.

Cheese Topped Black-Eyed Pea Casserole

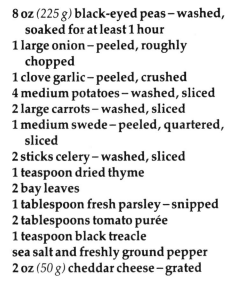

8 oz *(225 g)* black-eyed peas – washed, soaked for at least 1 hour
1 large onion – peeled, roughly chopped
1 clove garlic – peeled, crushed
4 medium potatoes – washed, sliced
2 large carrots – washed, sliced
1 medium swede – peeled, quartered, sliced
2 sticks celery – washed, sliced
1 teaspoon dried thyme
2 bay leaves
1 tablespoon fresh parsley – snipped
2 tablespoons tomato purée
1 teaspoon black treacle
sea salt and freshly ground pepper
2 oz *(50 g)* cheddar cheese – grated

Oven: 350°f, 180°c, G.M.4

1 Put the black-eyed peas and their soaking water into a saucepan. Cover and bring to the boil, reduce the heat and simmer for 20 minutes. When the time is up, drain, but reserve the cooking liquid.

2 Heat a small amount of oil in a large saucepan. Soften the onion and garlic. When the onion is transparent, add all the other vegetables. Cover and cook gently for about 10 minutes.

3 When the vegetables are beginning to soften, remove from the heat.

4 Remove the slices of potato, put to one side. Put the other vegetables, herbs and cooked peas into an ovenproof dish.

5 Make up the cooking liquid to 1 pint (575 ml) if necessary. Add the treacle and tomato purée, pour over the vegetables.

6 Arrange the slices of potatoes on the top.

Bake for an hour by which time the vegetables should be soft. Once cooked, put the grated cheese on the top, return to the oven and cook until the cheese browns.

An alternative would be to put the dish under a hot grill which would bubble the cheese more quickly.

Chilli without Carne

1 medium aubergine – washed, thinly sliced
salt
1 onion – peeled, roughly chopped
oil
12 oz *(350 g)* brown lentils – sorted, washed
½ teaspoon chilli powder
15 oz *(425 g)* tinned tomatoes
3 tablespoons tomato purée
¾ pt *(425 ml)* vegetable stock
4 oz *(125 g)* cooked kidney beans (or ½ tin)

1 Put the aubergine into a bowl, sprinkle each layer generously with salt, this is to remove the bitter juice of the aubergine (the process is known as degorging). Leave to stand for at least 30 minutes. Rinse under the cold tap to remove the salt then squeeze thoroughly, dry on kitchen paper.

2 Heat a little oil in a saucepan, soften the onion and garlic until the onion is transparent. Add the aubergine, chilli and lentils, stir well and cook for 4–5 minutes, stir occasionally to stop ingredients sticking to the pan.

3 Add the tomatoes, purée and stock, bring to the boil then simmer until the liquid has thickened. The slower this can be done the better, as it will give the flavours a chance to develop.

4 Add the cooked kidney beans and allow them to heat through before serving.

Serve with wholewheat bread or rice for a complete protein meal.

Butter Bean Flan

Pastry:
6 oz *(175 g)* wholewheat flour
3 oz *(75 g)* butter or margarine
a pinch of salt
3–4 tablespoons of water

Filling:
4 oz *(125 g)* cooked butter beans
2 tablespoons homemade tomato
   sauce (if available)
4 eggs
8 oz *(225 g)* cottage cheese
salt and freshly ground pepper

Decoration:
4 slices green pepper
4 slices red pepper

Oven: 425°f, 220°c, G.M.7

1 Make the pastry: Rub the fat into the flour and salt until it
   resembles fine breadcrumbs. Gradually add enough water to
   bring the ingredients together into a soft ball.

2 On a lightly floured surface with a floured rolling pin, roll out
   the pastry in a circle big enough to line an 8" (20 cm) flan tin.

3 Flip one end of the pastry over the rolling pin, pick up the dough
   and lay it over the tin. Gently push it down to the bottom of the
   tin, trim away the unwanted pastry from the edge with a knife.
   Prick all over the bottom of the tin with a fork, this will stop
   bubbles appearing in the case during cooking.

4 Bake blind: Cover the pastry with a sheet of greaseproof paper,
   weight this down with a pad of tin foil or some dried pulse. Bake
   for 10 minutes. By baking blind the finished flan will have a nice
   crisp bottom rather than a soggy one.

5 Once the case is cooked, remove the paper and beans or foil
   (these can be used again for baking blind so keep separately
   from your other pulses) leave the case to cool slightly.

6 Spread 2 good tablespoons of tomato sauce on the bottom of the
   case. Put the butter beans on top.

7 Beat the eggs, season with salt and pepper, stir in the cottage

cheese, and pour on top of the beans. Arrange the peppers in alternate colours on the top.

Bake for about 20–25 minutes until the egg has set and the top is golden brown.

This flan is really quick to make if you have the beans already cooked so this is a good reason to cook a few extra each time you are using butter beans.

Butter Bean Moussaka

8 oz *(225 g)* butter beans – washed, soaked
1 medium aubergine – washed, thinly sliced
1 large onion – peeled, roughly chopped
1 clove garlic – peeled, crushed
15 oz *(425 g)* tinned tomatoes
1 tablespoon tomato purée
4 oz *(125 g)* mushrooms – wiped, sliced
1 teaspoon oregano
1 teaspoon marjoram
salt and freshly ground pepper
oil

Topping:
2 tablespoons wholewheat flour
2 eggs
½ pt *(275 ml)* yoghurt
1 oz *(25 g)* hard cheese eg. cheddar – grated

Oven: 350°f, 180°c, G.M.4

1 Put the butter beans with their soaking water in a saucepan, cover and bring to the boil, reduce heat and simmer until cooked, approximately 2–2½ hours. Drain and put to one side.

2 Place the sliced aubergine in a bowl layered with plenty of salt to remove the bitter juice. This must be left to soak for at least 30 minutes.

3 Soften the onion and the garlic in a saucepan with a little oil until the onion is transparent.

4 Rinse the salt off the aubergine under the cold tap, squeeze out well, add to the onion together with the tomatoes, purée, mushrooms and herbs. Simmer gently until the aubergine is soft (15–20 minutes). Season with salt and pepper.

5 Put the aubergine mixture in the bottom of an ovenproof dish, layer the butter beans on the top.

6 Make the yoghurt topping: Stir the flour into the yoghurt, break the eggs into the mixture, stir well to make sure the ingredients are combined, season with salt and pepper, pour over the beans.

7 Grate the cheese over the top.

Bake for about 30 minutes until the top is bubbling and golden brown.

Aduki Bake

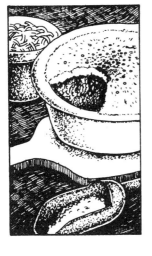

8 oz *(225 g)* aduki beans – washed,
  soaked
1 onion – peeled, thinly sliced
1 small leek – washed, thinly sliced
½ red pepper – washed, deseeded,
  roughly cubed
½ green pepper – washed, deseeded,
  roughly cubed
15 oz *(425 g)* tinned tomatoes
salt and freshly ground pepper
1 teaspoon thyme
1 tablespoon Worcester sauce
oil

Topping:
2 x ½ inch slices wholewheat bread –
  made into crumbs
1 oz *(25 g)* butter or margarine
1 teaspoon sesame seeds

Oven: 350°f, 180°c, G.M.4

1 Put the aduki beans and their soaking water in a saucepan, cover and bring to the boil, reduce the heat and simmer until tender, about 1 hour.

2 In a saucepan, soften the onion, leek and peppers in a little oil.

3 When the onion is transparent add the tomatoes, thyme and Worcester sauce, simmer until thick then season with salt and pepper.

4 Add the cooked, drained aduki beans to the sauce, check the seasoning, add more salt, pepper or Worcester sauce if needed. Transfer to an ovenproof dish. The dish can be left at this point for assembly at a later time.

5 Put the breadcrumbs on the top in an even layer. Divide the butter or margarine into pea size bits, dot over the top of the breadcrumbs, sprinkle with the sesame seeds.

Bake for 25–30 minutes until nutty brown.

Mung Bean Stir Fry

8 oz *(225 g)* mung beans – washed, soaked
1 medium leek – washed, finely sliced
½ red pepper – washed, deseeded, thinly sliced
½ green pepper – washed, deseeded, thinly sliced
2 sticks celery – washed
4 medium carrots – washed
4 oz *(125 g)* cashew nuts
½ inch root ginger – peeled
2 tablespoons Tamari (Soy) sauce
oil

1 Put the mung beans and their soaking water into a saucepan, cover, bring to the boil then simmer until cooked, about 40 minutes. Drain.

2 Put the sliced leek and peppers in a bowl.

3 Top and tail the carrots, cut into about 1½ inch sections. Cut into three lengthways, then slice into match stick size strips. Put with the other vegetables.

4 Cut the celery into 1½ inch pieces, slice lengthways in a similar size to the carrots. Put with the other vegetables.

5 Finely chop the root ginger, add to the vegetables, spoon over the Tamari sauce, cover and leave for 10–15 minutes.

6 Heat enough oil to just cover the bottom of a frying pan. When it is really hot add the vegetables, Tamari and cashew nuts, stir all the time. The cooking time is only a matter of minutes. Add the cooked mung beans and heat through for 1–2 minutes.

Serve immediately with rice for example.

Protein Pie

8 oz *(225 g)* yellow split peas – washed
1 large onion – peeled, roughly
   chopped
1 clove garlic – peeled, crushed
1 pt *(575 ml)* water
1 tablespoon oil
2 oz *(50 g)* oatmeal
8 oz *(225 g)* carrots – washed, coarsely
   grated
1 teaspoon thyme
1 teaspoon sage
salt and freshly ground pepper

Tomato sauce:
1 clove garlic – peeled, crushed
7 oz *(200 g)* tinned tomatoes
1 tablespoon tomato purée
1 bay leaf
½ teaspoon oregano
½ teaspoon basil
½ teaspoon thyme

Potato topping:
1½ lbs potatoes – washed
1 oz *(25 g)* butter or margarine
grated nutmeg
salt and freshly ground pepper

Oven: 375°f, 190°c, G.M.5

This is an attractive three layer dish which, as its name suggests is a complete protein meal all in one. It is colourful, full of flavour and texture and is straightforward to make.

1 Put the split peas, half the chopped onion, the garlic, water and oil in a saucepan, cover, bring to the boil then reduce heat and simmer for 20 minutes.
2 Add the oatmeal, stir well, cover and simmer for 10 minutes.
3 When the time is up, remove from the heat, add the grated carrot and herbs, season with salt and pepper. Transfer to an ovenproof dish.

4 Make the tomato sauce: soften the rest of the onion and the clove of garlic in a little oil until the onion is transparent. Add the rest of the ingredients, bubble quickly for about 5 minutes without a lid so the sauce will thicken. Season with salt and pepper. Put to one side.

5 Cook the potatoes: put the whole potatoes in a saucepan of cold salted water, cover, bring to the boil. Reduce the heat and simmer for 20 minutes or until the potatoes will easily slip off a knife. Drain.

6 Mash the potatoes with the fat, season with salt, pepper and nutmeg.

7 Assemble the dish: remove the bay leaf from the tomato sauce, spoon over the split pea mixture making an even layer, cover with the mashed potato. Smooth the top with a knife and mark in a criss-cross pattern, the top can be covered in a few dots of butter which will make a crunchy brown top.

Bake for 25–30 minutes until golden brown.

Haricot Bean Cobbler

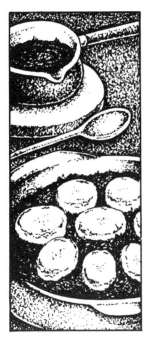

8 oz *(225 g)* haricot beans – washed, soaked
1 onion – peeled, thinly sliced
1 medium leek – washed, thinly sliced
½ red pepper – washed, deseeded, thinly sliced
½ green pepper – washed, deseeded, thinly sliced
1 oz *(25 g)* butter or margarine

White sauce:
  1 oz *(25 g)* potato flour (or wholewheat)
1 pt *(575 ml)* milk
1 teaspoon mixed herbs
salt and freshly ground pepper

Scone topping:
8 oz *(225 g)* wholewheat self raising flour (add 2 teaspoons baking powder if using plain flour)
2 oz *(50 g)* butter or margarine
1 teaspoon coriander – ground
1 teaspoon cumin – ground
pinch of salt, twists of pepper
8–10 tablespoons water

Oven: 400°f, 200°c, G.M.6

1 Put the beans and their soaking water in a saucepan, cover and bring to the boil, reduce the heat and simmer for 2 hours approximately until cooked. Once soft, drain.

2 In a saucepan, melt the fat, soften the vegetables, once the onions are transparent, add the potato flour, mix well, stir over the heat for a minute to make the roux.

3 Off the heat, gradually add the milk to the vegetables and roux, stir well, return to the heat, stir all the time until the sauce thickens. Add the mixed herbs, season with salt and pepper, remove from the heat.

4 Once the beans are cooked, add to the sauce, transfer to an ovenproof dish.

5 Make the scone topping: Rub the fat into the flour until it resembles breadcrumbs. Add the spices (and baking powder if used), season. Add enough water to form a soft dough so that all the ingredients come together into a ball. Divide the dough in half, then divide each half into 4 equal pieces, making 8 balls. Roll each piece between your palms, you might need to dust your hands with a little flour first, flatten slightly then place on top of the sauce.

Bake in the middle of the oven for 30 minutes. The scones will rise and the sauce will turn a golden brown.

Beans in Tomato Sauce

8 oz *(225 g)* haricot beans – washed, soaked
1 onion – peeled, roughly chopped
oil
tomato juice
1 teaspoon yeast extract
3 tablespoons tomato purée
salt and freshly ground pepper
Worcester sauce

1 Put the beans and their soaking water in a saucepan, cover and bring to the boil, simmer for about 2 hours until cooked. Once cooked, drain and reserve the liquid.

2 Make the cooking liquid up to 1½ pts (850 ml) with tomato juice, add the yeast extract and tomato purée to this.

3 Soften the onion in a little oil, once transparent add the tomato stock, cover, bring this to the boil then simmer without a lid to reduce the sauce a little, once it thickens after about 5–7 minutes, season to taste with salt and pepper and a good dash of Worcester sauce.

4 Add the cooked beans and warm through in the tomato sauce.

Serve with hot buttered toast for a complete and simple protein meal.

Grains

The term grain refers to the fruit of a cereal. The types that spring instantly to mind are wheat and rice, which are the two most commonly quoted examples because they make a major contribution to the world's diet today. In their natural state, that is to say, their whole form, they provide a rich source of B vitamins, protein and iron, and the outer coating or husk is a valuable source of all the important roughage that is so often missing in the modern refined diet. Both wholewheat and brown rice provide balanced foods in their own right. They contain starch for energy; vitamins and minerals in the correct proportions to help with the utilisation of that starch, and bran, which is vital to the movement of food through the system. It therefore stands to reason that if any of these components are removed or altered in any way, the whole balance will be upset and rendered useless.

The alternative is the processed variety, sliced white bread which bears more resemblance to a damp sponge, and white rice which has either been par-boiled, freeze-dried or converted into easy to cook rice. The amount of goodness remaining is questionable, but the rigours of a fast, modern, convenience-orientated life, demand such products, regardless of their lack of nutritional value. Or does it. . . .? Just like other wholefood ingredients, whole grains are much better for us and have a full, rich satisfying taste. They are also very quick and simple to use.

RICE

Brown rice still has the important germ and bran layer intact, which is present in the husk. It contains a high percentage of protein, very little fat and most of the vital B vitamins, particularly Thiamine and Nicotinic acid; both are needed for the utilisation of carbohydrates and the functioning of the nervous system. Large amounts of phosphorous and potassium are also present with iron for the blood and calcium which is necessary for healthy bones and teeth.

During the production of white rice, the grains are polished, which removes the husk coating, and therefore most of the goodness as well: as much as half of the mineral content, a little protein, some fat, and most of the B vitamins, not to mention nearly all the roughage or fibre. As with other refined products, some manufacturers attempt to replace what they have removed by adding chemical substitutes, then label it enriched and con the public into believing that they are eating good, wholesome food. Usually in this polished type of rice it is the Thiamine that is replaced in a synthesised form, but these B vitamins work together in an intricate fashion so it is doubtful if the addition does any good. Yet again it is a case of why not eat the natural product in the first place? At least you will be enjoying a product with a distinctive nutty flavour of its own, with a firm almost chewy texture, unlike white rice which is not exactly bulging with taste and acts as a rather bland accompaniment to spicy dishes such as curry and chilli. There is no chance of being left with a white gluey mound on your plate either, because whilst white rice is susceptible to bad cooking, brown rice is much easier to cook. Simply bring salted water to the boil, add the rice and simmer for 45 minutes until cooked. The end product does not have to be rinsed in hot water to stop it sticking together as with white rice, which in turn must wash away any remaining goodness.

Types of Rice
LONG GRAIN: this is a long, thin, oval shaped grain, used for savoury dishes, soups, salads and as an accompaniment to main meals. Remember, rice and pulses make a COMPLETE protein.
SHORT GRAIN: this has a slightly lighter flavour and so is more suitable for pudding dishes as the grains tend to remain separate even if they are cooked for a long time as in the case of rice pudding.

Buying and Storage
In terms of convenience, it is probably easier to buy short grain rice and use it for all your rice dishes, but if you only use rice in savoury dishes it is best to use the long grain variety. Organic rice is available in most wholefood shops. This really is the best buy as it is grown without the use of chemicals, but it will be slightly more expensive.

Rice will keep for as long as six months in a dry, air-tight container, without losing any nutritional value, which makes it a good item to buy in bulk, especially as its versatility makes it a useful food to have in an emergency. It takes no time to fling a few left-over bits and pieces into a pan with some rice and stock, and, in a short time you will have a risotto or savoury rice dish for those unexpected guests.

Cooking
Both types of rice are easy to cook, however, they do take a little longer than the white rice.

a) BOILING: Bring a pan of salted water to the boil, add the rice; approximately half a pound (225 g) for four people. Stir once, cover and simmer for about 45 minutes. Test after 35 minutes to see if it is ready. When it is cooked, it will be just soft to the bite, and slightly chewy in texture. Drain and serve immediately. For rice salad, cook in this way, drain and refresh the rice by running it under the cold tap. This stops any further cooking.

b) STEAMING: This is a good way of adding flavour during cooking. Heat some oil in a pan (you could add a little root ginger or garlic at this stage, just to flavour the oil, but remove it before you add the other ingredients), fry any vegetables and add any spices to be used. Stir the rice in the oil until it is well coated, cook for one minute. Pour one pint (575 ml) of vegetable stock over the rice, season and bring to the boil. Cover and reduce the heat. Cook for 45 minutes without lifting the lid to see what is happening. When the time is up, turn the heat off, but leave the dish untouched for a further ten minutes. By this time, the rice will have become moist and glossy as it sits in the steam.

c) BAKED: The end result using this method is richer in flavour and is an economical way of cooking rice if you already have the oven on. Cook as for steamed rice, sautéing the vegetables, adding the rice, then coating it in the oil. Transfer to an ovenproof dish, add stock that must be boiling and any herbs or spices, then cover and bake in a moderate oven for 45 minutes. Leave to stand for 10 minutes. A Middle Eastern addition to rice cooked in this fashion is dried fruits and various nuts which makes an interesting change, not to mention a complete protein!

WHEAT

Like rice, wheat is also packed full of goodness, and contains bran, that well-known source of fibre. Also endosperm which makes up the main body of the grain, and is white in appearance consisting mainly of starch. Finally, there is a small but very important element, the germ. This is nearly the most valuable part of the grain as it is here that the vitamins and minerals are to be found. The germ is packed full of most of the B vitamins, large amounts of vitamin E which is vital for the skin, and minerals such as calcium, potassium, iron, copper and magnesium. A little fat is present and far more protein than the endosperm, despite the vast difference in size.

Flour Milling
Most of the wheat grown goes towards making white flour. Here, the grain is ground on large metal rollers, the bran is removed and sold separately as animal fodder or back to the public. The germ is removed and again, sold back to the public at a higher price. The germ is removed because it includes a percentage of fat. This has a tendency to go rancid and will affect the shelf life of the product. One of the requirements of refined products is that they last a good length of time without deteriorating, hence the abundance of preservatives, stabilisers and anti-oxidants to be found in such products. The flour has now reached a creamy-white stage, it can be sold at this point and is called unbleached white flour. To achieve the familiar brilliant white colour, the flour undergoes bleaching with the help of a chemical called Chlorine Dioxide, which unfortunately also destroys the vitamin E. By the end of the process, none of the chemical will be left but it is true to say, the nutritional value of white flour will be sadly lacking.

There are nutritional standards laid down by most countries to ensure certain vitamin levels are maintained in white flour. As a result, the B vitamins Thiamine and Nicotinic acid are added and so is iron, but unfortunately this is in a form the body finds difficult to absorb. This problem is overcome by adding chalk, however this addition alters the calcium and phosphorus ratio, and so the somewhat depressing chain of events continues. The simple answer must be to eat wholewheat flour in the first place, with all the vitamins and minerals still intact together with the bran and wheatgerm which gives the flour the brown flecked appearance and the unmistakable nutty flavour.

Types of Flour

a) *Wholemeal, wholewheat, wholegrain:* These names are interchangable. Here the whole grain is used in the product.
b) *Stone ground:* Here the grain is milled between two mill stones, a practice that has been carried out for centuries. It is said that this method retains more of the goodness as the grains are not so heavily bruised.
c) *Organic flour:* Here the grain is grown and ground without the use of chemicals and so is a little more expensive.
d) *Strong flour:* This refers to the gluten content of the flour. Gluten is the nitrogenous part which remains in the form of a sticky substance when the starch is washed out of the flour and combines with the other ingredients being used. (This washing out of the starch is how sauces with a flour base thicken). Certain varieties of grain produce flour that has a higher than average gluten content so this is used in bread making where a strong structure is required. The softer flours, those without so much gluten are kept for cakes and pastries etc.
e) *81% and 85% Wholewheat flours:* This refers to the extraction of the bran. This type of flour has only the finer bran particles remaining and so is ideal for cakes and pastries etc. 100% flour with its coarser bran can be used for all types of cooking, it just does not give the light, more even texture of the other flours.
f) *Strong, unbleached white flour:* This flour is sold at the creamy white stage of the production cycle. Obviously it is better than the bleached flour, but, it does not have all the nutritional properties of the wholewheat flour.
g) *Brown Flours:* These are not 100% wholegrain flours, they are more likely to be 81% or 85% flours or at their worst, they could just be white flour that has been dyed brown: so do read the label.
   REMEMBER – 100%, 81% and 85% flours do contain wheatgerm which is where the vitamin E is stored. This is the bit that could go off, so avoid keeping this sort of flour for more than a month.
h) *Granary flour:* Here the whole grains of wheat or rye are

sprouted, then toasted and added to 81% or 85% flour. It does make a lovely loaf of bread and a nice change.

WHEAT PRODUCTS

Wheat Bran
The average daily roughage requirement can be obtained from 5 ounces (150 g) of wholemeal bread; the number of slices will depend on how thin or thick you cut them. If you feel you need a little extra roughage, bran could be the answer as it can be added to cereals, soups, stews etc. While I am talking about bran I will mention two fairly new products, oat bran and soya bran: these have a finer texture with a lovely nutty taste and certainly bear no resemblance to animal food. They make an interesting alternative which you might find more acceptable.

Wheatgerm
This is sold in a stabilised form which stops the product going rancid. Because it has been treated it is not quite as pure in this form, but is still full of protein, B vitamins and vitamin E, having an attractive nutty flavour. Again, it can be sprinkled over cereal, or put in cakes and bread. I use it to coat things like lentil patties as it gives a lovely even crunchy layer when cooked.

Wholewheat Grain (or Berries)
This product is readily available in the wholefood shops. It can be cooked in the same way as rice to give a nutty tasting alternative because when cooked, it becomes plump, round and moist. It can be used as a pudding, cooked in milk with honey, spices and fruit. Do not attempt this unless you have an Aga, because it takes 9 hours to cook, at a very low temperature. A nutritious way of using the whole grain is to sprout them for a short period of time, just until the sprout is the same length as the grain itself. By sprouting, the carbohydrate content will be reduced, the vitamin and mineral levels stay the same but vitamin C is created. If you are feeling really keen, you can make your own granary flour. Spread sprouted grains on a baking sheet and toast in a moderate oven for about 20 minutes. Leave to cool, then store in an airtight container. You will need to add 3 tablespoons for every pound (450 g) of strong wholegrain flour.

Cracked or Kibbled Wheat
This is just coarsely ground wheat grains, the type usually found on the top of loaves of bread. The grain can also be soaked and cooked like rice and served as an accompaniment.

Bulgar Wheat (Bulgur or Burghul)
The most common use for this is in the Middle Eastern dish Tabouli. The great thing is, it needs no cooking. It is soaked in either water or lemon juice, squeezed out and mixed with cubed cucumber, tomato and chopped mint or parlsey, then tossed in a dressing. It makes a very interesting, tasty and easy to prepare salad. I quite often top it with a garlic and yoghurt dressing, decorated with more diced cucumber. It needs no cooking because the wheat grains are soaked and then toasted until they crack.

Wholewheat Pasta
This is made from Durum wheat, the same as white pasta. This type of flour is particularly high in protein. Wholewheat pasta comes in all shapes and sizes, and in many of the larger supermarkets you will have the choice of fresh and dried. It is cooked in the same way as the white, in salted boiling water with a splash of oil to add flavour and prevent sticking. Fresh pasta will only take a few minutes to reach the *'al dente'* stage, whereas the dried takes 15–20 minutes. *Al dente* means 'to the teeth' or just cooked and the term applies to many items not just pasta.

Wholewheat Semolina
Semolina is made from coarsely ground Durum wheat, so it is basically a coarse flour. It is probably best known for the milk pudding served with jam. I wonder how many people have been put off this because of the stodge provided for school lunch? It can be combined with milk and cheese to make a thick paste which is the shallow fried and served with a herby tomato sauce. This is called Gnocchi (pronounced Knocky) and makes a lovely supper dish. It can also be used in the same way as Bulgar. It does not have to be soaked, but can be mixed straight away with the dressing and left to stand for half an hour or so until all the liquid is absorbed.

WHOLE OATS

The most common use of oats is in porridge. It may look boring and stodgy, but it is packed with protein and thiamine, containing only a little fat and also significant amounts of iron and potassium. What a wonderful way to start the day.

Oats and oat products like the ones listed below have a variety of uses such as for flapjacks and other biscuits, for crumble toppings and in coatings for croquettes and burgers etc.

a) OATMEAL. This is basically whole oats that have been ground to different degrees to give fine, medium and coarse grained oatmeal. Fine and medium are used in biscuits and griddle cakes like Bannock cakes which are traditional Scottish oatcakes cooked on a heavy griddle iron (a flat dish heated directly on the hob). These are eaten hot with butter, honey, jam or cheese. The coarse oatmeal is best for porridge, it needs to be soaked overnight as otherwise it takes ages to cook.

b) ROLLED OATS (JUMBO OATS). Also called oat flakes, they make up the basic bulk ingredient in the muesli base. They are produced when the whole grain is softened by steam, rolled and then cooled and dried. This is a better product than –

c) QUICK PORRIDGE OATS. These are rolled and partially cooked before the final cooling and drying.These flakes are smaller than jumbo oats.

RYE

Rye is usually used as a flour for bread. It makes a light or dark coloured loaf. The dough is heavier than the wholemeal, but it does have a lovely flavour. Rye has a similar nutritional value to wholewheat as far as fat and thiamine are concerned, but has less protein and nicotinic acid and more riboflavin. It is therefore a good idea to mix the two together. Rye flakes are often found in the base of muesli.

BARLEY

Probably the best known example is Pearl Barley as used in soups and broths. In nutritional terms, this is on the same level as the white rice, that is to say, it has been polished. The whole grain version is called POT barley and contains protein and thiamine. It can be cooked in the same way as brown rice and takes the same length of time. It makes a good addition to vegetable casseroles or stews as it has thickening properties, and it imparts a rich flavour.

You can also buy barley flour which, when added to wholewheat bread flour gives a certain sweetness to the loaf – the final product has a soft texture too.

Barley flakes are sold, and yes, you've guessed it, they can be added to the muesli base.

MALT EXTRACT

A surprising product of barley is malt. It is a sticky, dark brown syrup, packed full of protein, B vitamins, iron, calcium, potassium and lots of natural sugar. It is an acquired taste, but it is only usually used in small quantities, mainly in yeast cookery, as it reacts well with yeast enzymes. Malt bread with sultanas is a family favourite at tea time.

MILLET

This is not an every day sort of grain. It is high in protein, calcium and iron with the B vitamins, thiamine and riboflavin, together with nicotinic acid. It cooks very quickly, makes an interesting change from rice and can be added to other dishes, such as casseroles or stews.

BUCKWHEAT

This is expensive compared with other grains, basically because it is difficult to get hold of. The tiny brown seeds have to be removed from the husk, but it is well worth the effort as the final product is high in protein, minerals and vitamins. It has a strong nutty flavour, and is grey and flecked in appearance. It has no gluten content so the uses are limited. The best use is in pancakes served with vegetables, or pulses topped with a sauce, sour cream or yoghurt.

Jumbo Crunch

4 tablespoons sunflower oil
8 oz *(225 g)* honey
1 lb *(450 g)* jumbo oats
4 oz *(125 g)* mixed nuts
2 oz *(50 g)* sultanas
1 tablespoon sesame seeds
1 tablespoon sunflower seeds

Oven: 350°f, 180°c, G.M.4

1 Warm the oil and honey in a roasting tin. A tip for weighing out the honey is to sprinkle the scale pan with some flour, spoon the honey onto this then it will easily tip off into the roasting tin.

2 Add the other ingredients except the sultanas and stir thoroughly so everything is evenly coated with honey.

3 Cook until nicely browned, for approximately 20 minutes. Turn regularly to ensure even browning.

4 Add the sultanas just before the end, otherwise they become like little bullets.

Once cooked, leave to cool then store in an air-tight container. This makes a lovely breakfast cereal served with milk, or combine with fresh or stewed fruit and yoghurt for a delicious quick pudding.

Soup Mix Soup

5 oz *(150 g)* soup mix – washed, soaked for 1 hour
1 medium carrot – washed, thinly sliced
1 medium onion – peeled, roughly chopped
1 stick celery – washed, sliced
oil
vegetable stock
bay leaf

1 Soften the vegetables in a little oil in a covered saucepan until the onion is transparent.

2 Drain the water off the soup mix, reserve this liquid and make it up to 2 pts (1.1 l) with vegetable stock.

3 Turn the soup mix in the oil and softened vegetables, and cook for a minute.

4 Add the stock and bay leaf, cover and bring to the boil then simmer gently until the pulses and grains are soft (this takes 35–60 minutes).

Season with salt and freshly ground black pepper.

- This is a quick simple complete protein meal in a bowl as the soup mix contains cereal flakes such as oat and barley and pulses like split peas and black-eyed peas.

Gnocchi with Tomato Sauce

1 pt *(570 ml)* milk
1 onion – peeled, sliced
1 clove (or pinch of ground cloves)
1 bay leaf
parsley stalks
4 oz *(125 g)* wholewheat semolina
6 oz *(175 g)* strong hard cheese e.g. Cheddar, Sage Derby – grated
a pinch of mustard powder (or a teaspoon of made mustard)
a pinch of cayenne
1 tablespoon freshly chopped parsley

Coating:
1 beaten egg
oatmeal
oil

1 Put the milk in a saucepan with the onion, clove, bay leaf and parsley stalks. Heat gently for 7 minutes to 'infuse' the flavours into the milk.

2 Strain the milk, return to the saucepan and bring to the boil, tip in the semolina, stirring all the time until it becomes thick. It is important that the milk is at boiling point otherwise the semolina will not thicken.

3 Once cooked and thick, remove from the heat. Add the cheese, parsley, mustard, season with cayenne , salt and pepper.

4 Run a dinner plate under the cold tap, shake off the excess water. Spread the semolina and cheese mixture into a round. Put in the fridge to chill for at least 30 minutes. (As an alternative, you can cut the mixture out into shapes with a pastry cutter then place in the fridge).

5 Once cold, divide the mixture into 8 equal wedges, chill again if it is still a bit soft.

6 Coat the Gnocchi: First put the beaten egg into a flat dish, and onto a plate sprinkle an even layer of oatmeal.
Dip the wedges in the egg wash so they are completely covered then turn each piece in the oatmeal until well sealed.

7 Heat some oil in a saucepan until a blue haze appears, this will tell you that the fat is hot enough.

8 Reduce the heat slightly, shallow fry the Gnocchi on one side. When golden brown (3–4 minutes) turn over and cook the other side. Do not overcrowd the pan as this will make turning difficult and will reduce the heat in the pan so instead of browning and crisping up the Gnocchi will absorb the oil.

Serve with homemade tomato sauce.

Oatmeal and Vegetable Scramble

Oven: 350°f, 180°c, G.M.4

4 oz *(125 g)* oatmeal (coarse or medium)
1 pt *(575 ml)* vegetable stock (Vecon or Yeast extract)
2 medium leeks – washed, sliced thinly
1 large carrot – washed, sliced thinly
1 onion – peeled, sliced
2 sticks celery – washed, sliced thinly
½ red pepper – washed, deseeded, sliced
½ green pepper – washed, deseeded, sliced
oil
salt and freshly ground pepper
1 teaspoon mixed herbs
4 tomatoes – washed, sliced (or homemade tomato sauce)

Topping:
5 eggs – beaten
a knob of butter
1 dessertspoon of milk per egg used
¼ teaspoon mixed herbs

1 Bring the stock to the boil in a saucepan. Once it is bubbling, add the oatmeal, stir and cook until it comes back to the boil and thickens, then remove from the heat.

2 In another saucepan, soften the vegetables in a little oil. Cover and cook for about 10 minutes until they are soft.

3 Stir the vegetables into the oatmeal, season with salt and pepper and the mixed herbs. Transfer to an ovenproof dish.

4 Arrange the slices of tomato (or spread the tomato sauce) over the top of the oatmeal layer.

5 Make the topping: Melt the butter in a saucepan add the milk and the beaten egg, season well with the herbs, salt and pepper. Stir over a gentle heat until they just begin to scramble. Spoon over the tomato layer.

Bake for 20–30 minutes until the egg sets and browns slightly.

Macaroni Special

5 oz *(150 g)* wholewheat macaroni
1 medium onion – peeled, roughly
   chopped
1 clove garlic – peeled, crushed
1 tablespoon curry powder
8 oz *(225 g)* red lentils – sorted,
   washed
1 medium cooking apple – washed,
   cored, roughly chopped
1 small green pepper – washed,
   deseeded, chopped
1 pt *(575 ml)* vegetable stock
½ lemon – juice
salt and freshly ground pepper
2 tablespoons mango chutney
3 tomatoes – washed, roughly
   chopped

Sauce for the topping:
1 oz *(25 g)* butter or margarine
1 oz *(25 g)* wholewheat flour
1 pt *(575 ml)* milk
salt and freshly ground pepper
1 teaspoon good mustard
1 oz *(25 g)* cheese – grated

Oven: 350°f, 180°c, G.M.4

1 Make the lentil base: Gently soften the vegetables in a little oil.
   When the onion is transparent add the curry powder and cook
   for a few minutes. Add the lentils and turn well in the oil, cook
   for a further few minutes.

2 Add the stock, salt, pepper and lemon juice, simmer until all the
   liquid has been absorbed, so do not cover.

3 Stir in the mango chutney and the tomato, transfer to an
   ovenproof dish.

4 Cook the macaroni: Bring a saucepan of salted water to the boil,
   once it is bubbling add the macaroni, half put the lid back on
   and simmer for 10 minutes or until just cooked. Drain and leave
   on one side.

5 Make the white sauce: melt the fat in a saucepan, add the flour to form a roux, stir over the heat and cook for a minute. Remove from the heat to add the milk, mix well, return to the heat and allow to thicken. Add the salt, pepper and mustard, stir in the macaroni and pour onto the lentil base.

6 Sprinkle the cheese on the top.

Bake for 30–35 minutes until the top is golden brown.

Whole-wheat Grain Salad

8 oz (225 g) wholewheat grain – soaked overnight
1 red pepper – washed, deseeded, cubed small
¼ cucumber – cubed small
1 tablespoon white wine vinegar
3 tablespoons oil
sea salt and freshly ground pepper
1 teaspoon concentrated mint sauce

1 Put the wholewheat and the soaking water into a saucepan, cover and bring to the boil. Reduce the heat and simmer gently until the grain is tender, (this takes approximately an hour). Drain.

2 Mix all the other ingredients together and add to the wholewheat, leave to cool.

This makes a fresh looking and tasty salad. The wholewheat has a lovely nutty flavour which goes well with the tangy dressing and the crunchy vegetables, making a nice change from rice salad.

Whole-wheat Pancakes with Spicy Chick Peas

Pancake mix:
4 oz *(125 g)* wholewheat flour
a pinch of salt
1 egg
½ pt *(275 ml)* milk

Chick Pea filling:
8 oz *(225g)* chick peas – washed, soaked
1 medium onion – peeled, roughly chopped
1 clove garlic – peeled, crushed
oil
1 teaspoon cumin seeds (or ground)
1 teaspoon ground coriander
1 teaspoon ground paprika
a good pinch of cayenne
¼ pt *(150 ml)* cooking liquid
3 tablespoons tomato purée
2 tomatoes – washed, roughly chopped

Decoration:
2 tomatoes – washed, roughly chopped
1 oz *(25 g)* Cheddar – grated

Oven: 325°f, 170°c, G.M.3

1 Put the chick peas and the soaking water into a saucepan, cover, bring to the boil, reduce the heat and simmer until soft, for approximately 2 hours. Drain when cooked, but keep ¼ pt (150 ml) of the liquid.

2 Make the sauce: Soften the onion and garlic with the spices in a little oil over a low heat. Cook until the onions are transparent.

3 Stir in the tomato purée and the cooking liquid, simmer gently for a few minutes.

4 Add the chick peas, cover and continue to simmer for 15–20 minutes over a low heat. The chick pea filling can always be made well in advance and left to cool.

5 Make the pancake batter: Put the flour and salt into a bowl, make a dip in the centre, break the egg into this, gradually add the milk, stir all the time. The finished batter should be of a pouring consistency. Leave to stand for at least 10 minutes.

6 Cook the pancakes: Heat some oil in a small frying pan, when a blue haze appears, the oil is hot enough. Pour off some of the oil into an ovenproof dish, leaving about a teaspoonful in the pan.

7 Turn the heat down to moderate, add two good tablespoons of batter, swirl the pan around to make a thin pancake. Once the batter has set (2–3 minutes) turn the pancake over using a palette knife, the lacy pattern now showing is the right side. Cook the other side for 1–2 minutes.

8 Layer the cooked pancakes on top of each other on a plate, leave in a warm place.

9 After each pancake, heat the pan again with a teaspoon of oil before adding the next amount of batter.

10 Add the chopped tomato to the chick pea filling.

11 Using a circular flan dish or pie plate layer up the pancakes alternately with the chick pea filling ending up with a pancake on the top.

12 Put the remaining two chopped tomatoes on the top of the pancake, sprinkle with the grated cheese.

Bake in the oven for 25–30 minutes until the cheese is bubbling and brown and the filling is hot.

Serve with extra tomato sauce if desired, decorated with chopped parsley.

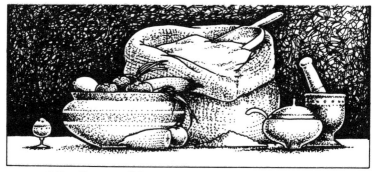

Tabouli (Tabbouleh)

4 oz *(125 g)* cracked wheat (Bulgar wheat)

2 tomatoes – washed, quartered, deseeded, cubed

2 spring onions – washed, thinly sliced

3 tablespoons oil

salt and freshly ground pepper

½ cucumber – washed, cube the same size as the tomato

a squeeze of lemon juice

1 dessertspoon mint sauce concentrate (or fresh chopped mint)

a good handful of chopped parsley

1 Put the cracked wheat in a large bowl, cover generously with cold water and leave for about an hour by which time it will have doubled in size.

2 Drain any excess water from the wheat. Tip into a clean tea towel, gather up the edges and squeeze firmly to remove as much liquid as possible.

3 Transfer the wheat to a tray, spread out to dry off a bit more.

4 Mix the vegetables with the oil, lemon juice and mint, season to taste.

5 Combine the vegetable vinaigrette with the now dry wheat. Transfer to a clean bowl and decorate with the parsley.

This is delicious by itself or served with Tzatsiki.

Seedy Brown Rice

2 tablespoons oil
1 tablespoon sesame seeds
1 tablespoon sunflower seeds
1 large onion – peeled, roughly
 chopped
1 teaspoon ground cumin
8 oz *(225 g)* long grain brown rice
1 pt *(575 ml)* vegetable stock
1 bay leaf
salt and freshly ground pepper

1 Heat the oil in a saucepan. Soften the onion with the seeds, turn regularly so the seeds brown evenly.

2 When the onion is transparent add the cumin and rice and cook for a couple of minutes.

3 Add the stock and the bay leaf, cover, bring to the boil, stir once, then cover again, reduce the heat and simmer for 35–40 minutes.

4 Cook for a further 5 minutes without the lid if all the liquid has not been absorbed. Remove the bay leaf. Season with salt and pepper.

By adding the seeds to the rice in this way makes the rice of more benefit to the body.

This makes an excellent accompaniment to all dishes as the combination of the seeds and rice is a complete protein.

Demerara Chocolate Sponge With Mocha Sauce

Sponge:
4 oz *(125 g)* butter or margarine
4 oz *(125 g)* golden granulated sugar
4 oz *(125 g)* wholewheat self raising
   flour (add 1 teaspoon of baking
   powder if using plain)
2 teaspoons carob powder
1 tablespoon milk
a few drops of natural vanilla essence
   (optional)
Demerara sugar

Mocha sauce:
½ pt *(275 ml)* milk
1 tablespoon cornflour
1 tablespoon golden granulated
   sugar
2 teaspoons carob powder
1 teaspoon instant coffee

Oven: 375°f, 190°c, G.M.5

1 Beat the fat and sugar together until they are light, soft and
   fluffy.
2 Add the eggs with the flour and carob powder gradually beating
   well after each addition.
3 Add enough milk to make the mixture a soft dropping
   consistency, add the vanilla essence.
4 Grease an 8" (20 cm) cake tin or a pie dish, spoon the sponge
   mixture in and smooth the top. Sprinkle liberally with demerara
   sugar for a crunchy top.
Bake for 25–30 minutes until well risen and firm to the touch.

Mocha sauce:
1 Heat the milk in a saucepan over a gentle heat.
2 In a bowl combine the cornflour, sugar, carob and coffee with a
   little of the warming milk.
3 When the milk nears boiling point, remove from the heat, stir
   into the sauce mix, when well combined return to the saucepan.
   Cook over a gentle heat until the sauce thickens.

Steamed Maple and Walnut Sponge

4 oz *(125 g)* **butter or margarine**
4 oz *(125 g)* **Barbados sugar**
6 oz *(175 g)* **wholewheat self raising flour (use 2 teaspoons of baking powder if using plain flour)**
2 oz *(50 g)* **walnuts – roughly chopped**

Grease the inside of a pudding basin (1½ pt) with a light flavoured oil or with margarine.

1 Put the steamer saucepan on to boil.
2 Beat (cream) the fat and sugar together until soft and light and fluffy in texture.
3 Add the eggs and flour (with baking powder if used) combine really well. Add the nuts, mix well.
4 Spoon the maple syrup into the bottom of the pudding basin, place the sponge mixture on the top, smooth evenly.
5 Grease or brush a sheet of greaseproof paper with oil, make an inch pleat in the middle of the paper. Put the greased side down on the top of the bowl, secure with string or a rubber band.
6 Place the basin in the steamer compartment of the double boiler.
Cook for 1½–2 hours.
The water must boil fast throughout the steaming, if not the pudding might be 'soggy' or only partially cooked.
NEVER let the water go off the boil, it only needs to be a gentle bubbling and keep an eye on the level of the water so the pan does not boil dry.

To serve – remove the paper, place a warm plate on the top of the bowl, holding the plate and the bowl together, turn the bowl upside down. The pudding should slip onto the plate, if not give it a sharp tap and a shake.

Treacle Tart

8 oz *(225 g)* wholewheat flour
4 oz *(125 g)* margarine or butter
3–4 tablespoons water
a pinch of salt

Filling:
6 oz *(175 g)* wholewheat breadcrumbs
1 lemon – zest and juice
3–4 tablespoons black treacle
3–4 tablespoons runny honey

Oven: 400°f, 200°c, G.M.6

1 Put 2 metal tablespoons to warm, this way the treacle will slip off more easily, so measuring is more accurate.

2 Make the pastry: Rub the fat into the flour and salt until it resembles fine breadcrumbs. Add enough water to make a soft dough. Roll out the pastry on a lightly floured surface in a circle big enough to line an 8" (20 cm) flan tin, flan ring or pie plate. Trim away the unwanted edges, and prick the bottom of the pastry case with a fork.

3 Put the breadcrumbs into the case, sprinkle with the lemon juice and zest.

4 Using the warm spoon, drizzle the black treacle over the crumbs followed by the honey (using a clean spoon!) The filling needs to be fairly moist.

Bake for 30–35 minutes until the pastry is golden brown and the top is becoming crunchy.

The tart is best eaten warm, because as it cools the treacle will become firmer, it re-heats very well.

Serve with custard, cream or yoghurt.

Mincemeat Tart

Pastry:
8 oz *(225 g)* wholewheat flour
4 oz *(125 g)* butter or margarine
a pinch of salt
3–4 tablespoons water

Mincemeat:
1 oz *(25 g)* dried dates
1 oz *(25 g)* butter
5 tablespoons water
½ teaspoon mixed spice
1 teaspoon ground mace
1 teaspoon ground cinnamon
1 teaspoon ground cloves
grated nutmeg
½ teaspoon ground allspice
1 medium cooking apple – washed, grated
1 lemon – zest and juice
8 oz *(225 g)* sultanas and raisins – mixed
3 oz *(75 g)* currants
1 oz *(25 g)* mixed peel
2 oz *(50 g)* whole almonds – roughly chopped
3 oz *(75 g)* Barbados sugar
2 tablespoons sherry (or brandy)

Oven: 375°f, 190°c, G.M.5

1 Make the pastry: Rub the fat into the flour and salt until it resembles fine breadcrumbs. Add enough water to bring all the ingredients together into a soft ball.

2 On a floured surface, using a floured rolling pin, roll the dough into a circle big enough to line an 8" flan ring or dish that has been lightly greased. Put the pastry into the tin, pushing it well down to the bottom. Trim the edges with a knife, put the remaining pastry to one side.

3 Make the mincemeat: Soften the dates in the water with the butter and spices in a saucepan over a low heat.

4 Combine the other ingredients together in a bowl.

5 When the dates are soft, stir into the other ingredients and mix well. Spoon into the pastry case.

6 Bring the pastry trimmings together into a ball and roll out. Cut strips long enough to go across the top of the tart. Moisten the edge of the pastry case with a little water and lay the strips across in a pattern. Stick them down firmly. Trim the edges.

Bake for 30–40 minutes until the pastry is golden brown.

If you want to keep the mincemeat for a couple of weeks before using it, reduce the amount of water in the recipe but increase the amount of alcohol, this will act as a preserving agent. Keeping the mincemeat will do wonders for the flavour.

Honey Oatties

3 oz *(75 g)* **butter or margarine**
4 oz *(125 g)* **wholewheat flour**
4 oz *(125 g)* **oatmeal**
3 tablespoons runny honey
½ teaspoon baking powder
¼ teaspoon salt

Oven: 375°f, 190°c, G.M.5

Grease a baking tin 10½" x 6½" (27 x 16 cm).

1 Rub the fat into the flour and oatmeal, add the salt and baking powder, mix well.

2 Spoon in the honey and mix thoroughly.

3 Press into the greased tin, smooth the surface with a knife.

Bake for 5–8 minutes until golden brown.

Divide into 16 fingers, cool briefly before removing from the tin, finish the cooling on a wire rack.

Dark Ginger-bread

8 oz *(225 g)* **Barbados sugar (or molasses sugar)**
6 oz *(175 g)* **butter or margarine**
12 oz *(350 g)* **black treacle**
½ pt *(275 ml)* **milk**
1 **egg**
1 lb *(450 g)* **wholewheat flour**
2 **teaspoons ground ginger**
2 **teaspoons baking powder**
½ **teaspoon bicarbonate of soda**
½ **teaspoon salt**

Oven: 350°f, 180°c, G.M.4

Grease a roasting tin and line with greaseproof paper.

1 Put the sugar, fat and syrup into a saucepan to melt. A tip for weighing out the syrup is to sprinkle flour over the pan of the scales, weigh out the treacle onto this, then tip the whole lot into the saucepan. (The little bit of extra flour will not make any difference).

2 Once everything has melted, remove from the heat and cool slightly, then stir in the milk.

3 Put the flour, ginger, baking powder and bicarbonate of soda into a bowl, gradually pour in the syrup mixture, and stir well to incorporate the ingredients.

4 Add the egg and beat the mixture. Tip into the prepared tin. Bake for about 1½ hours. Check after 1 hour, if it looks done, check by putting a knife into the middle of the cake, if this comes out clean it is cooked.

Plain Sponge Cake

6 oz *(175 g)* butter or margarine
6 oz *(175 g)* golden granulated or Demerara sugar
6 oz *(175 g)* wholewheat self raising flour (add 1½ teaspoons of baking powder if using plain flour)
3 eggs
3 tablespoons of jam

Oven: 350°f, 180°c, G.M.4

Grease two 8" (20 cm) sandwich tins, dust with flour, tip out the excess.

1 Beat (cream) the fat and sugar together until soft and light and fluffy in texture.

2 Add the eggs one at a time with a little of the flour to stop the eggs from curdling which sometimes happens if the eggs are added to the creamed mixture by themselves.

3 Beat in the rest of the flour. The mixture should be a dropping consistency, a little warm water can be added to achieve this.

4 Divide the mixture between the two tins, smooth the surface.

Bake for 30–35 minutes until brown on the top. Check to see if the cake is done by gently touching the centre of the cake, it should feel firm yet springy. Turn out of the tins and leave to cool on a cooling rack. Sandwich together with jam.

Variations:

A Add the zest of two lemons to the sponge mixture. Place the sponge into a deep 8" cake tin. Cook for about 40 minutes, check to see if done as above.

Turn the cake out of the tin and prick all over the top with a fork or skewer. Dissolve two tablespoons of golden granulated sugar in the juice of the lemons, pour this over the cake. Some will soak into the cake, the rest will crystallise on the top making a crunchy layer.

B The sandwich sponge can be filled with butter icing – cream 6 oz (175 g) of the granulated sugar (or Demerara sugar) with 4 oz (125 g) margarine, when this is soft, add 1–2 tablespoons of warm water, this will make the filling easier to spread. You can flavour this by adding coffee powder to the warm water, or carob powder in the same way for a chocolate flavour. Chopped nuts and the zests of oranges and lemons can also be used.

Basic Whole-wheat Shortcrust Pastry

8 oz *(225 g)* wholewheat flour
4 oz *(125 g)* butter or margarine
a pinch of salt
3–4 tablespoons cold water

The general idea is to use half the quantity of fat to flour, this will make all purpose pastry for flans, tarts, pies and pastries etc.

A point to remember when making pastry is to keep everything cool – fat, water, atmosphere, hands – all very well, but not always possible, so handle the pastry as little as possible to at least stop the heat from your hands melting the fat.

Once made, I roll mine out on a lightly floured surface, line the required container then leave it in the fridge for a while to relax. This will help to stop the pastry from shrinking once it goes into the oven.

1 Quickly and lightly rub the fat into the flour and salt using only your finger tips. Lift the mixture high above the bowl letting it drop back as you rub in. This way air is introduced which will make a light pastry.
2 Add enough water to bring all the ingredients together into a soft ball.
3 On a lightly floured surface, with a floured rolling pin, roll out the pastry, use as required.
4 Chill.
5 Bake in a pre-heated oven: 425°f, 220°c, G.M.7

Vegetables

Vegetables, the produce of field and garden, constitute a far more abundant and varied source of nourishment than most people imagine. By themselves, their protein levels are not vast but this is overcome by using them in conjunction with other food groups. Their value lies in their stores of essential minerals and vitamins together with important levels of roughage. When eaten with other foods they add a great deal of interest to a meal in the form of colour, texture and taste.

In the Middle East and Asia for example, they are a highly regarded food source, prized as highly as meat, and treated with great care and respect during preparation and cooking. The opposite in fact more often than not to the way vegetables are cooked in Western households. Here they are thought of as a second rate food, only fit to be served as a plain overcooked accompaniment to a meat dish.

Vegetables are a great source of inspiration. By altering the combinations and types of vegetables used, new dishes can be created with ease, and subtle alterations can change the whole character of the end result.

The wide choice available to us today is thanks to centuries of experiments with edible plants. The Romans were great gardeners, their major cities had market gardens growing amongst other things, lettuce and cucumbers – vegetables that had once been restricted to Asia Minor and India. As they colonised Europe they brought with them plants, roots and seeds introducing the natives in the northern lands to the delights of spinach, broccoli, asparagus, lettuce, cucumber and aubergine. Centuries later, the Spanish became another major influence. After conquering Central and Southern America, they returned home with a variety of plants and seeds. This was the start of tomatoes, sweet peppers, beans, sweetcorn and potatoes. With such a wealth of ingredients countries soon developed their own styles of cooking. For example in Asia the elegant style of concentrating on vegetables with the frugal use of meat was well under way as shown by the dish Iman Bayildi. (Aubergines are filled with a pine nut, tomato and green pepper stuffing, flavoured with garlic, olive oil and oregano).

Eventually, the hit and miss affair of cultivation was rationalised by the scientists. Haphazard plant breeding was replaced by plant genetics, first pioneered by the Austrian monk Mendel, in the 19th century. By the 20th century, healthy, sturdy plants could be ensured; being more resistant to disease, they had high yields of a first class quality. As a result of this type of work, new vegetables have been 'created'. Courgettes, as everyone knows, are just baby marrows, and mange tout, with their small tender peas and succulent pods are both a result of modern techniques of selection. They stem from plants bred so they will not grow to maturity.

VEGETABLES AND HEALTH

The role of the vegetable as a purveyor of health has been recognised ever since the days of early medicine men, who advised patients that vegetables could balance the 'humours' of their bodies; hence children are continually told to eat their greens!

Vegetables provide almost all of the specialised vitamins and minerals needed to keep us in good health, together with energy giving carbohydrates.

Green leafy vegetables are rich in the vitamins A, B and C and in the mineral calcium. Tubers and root vegetables, thought of more in terms of carbohydrates, are also rich in vitamins and minerals. For example, one medium sized potato supplies up to a third of the body's daily requirement of vitamin C.

Vegetables do not include all the amino acids needed to make them a good source of protein, so the best idea is to boost what is available by using them with milk based sauces, cheese, eggs, nuts, seeds or pulses.

BUYING

1. It is impossible to overstate the importance of freshness. As soon as the vegetable is harvested, nutrients and flavour will be lost, so always look for fresh, crisp looking items. If they look tired and limp in the shop, by the time you get around to using them at home, any remaining goodness will be very low.

2. Avoid packaged vegetables. Once they have been stored in plastic bags they deteriorate very quickly. If you have no choice, take them out of the bags as soon as you get home, and use as quickly as possible.
3. Seasonal vegetables will always be of better quality and price so make full use of what is available (see chart).
4. Do not stock up with vegetables (even if it does mean several shopping trips sometimes), especially the delicate ones. What happens is the plants continuing metabolic process will gradually cause loss of flavour. In peas and sweetcorn for example, natural sugars very quickly convert to less appetising starch. Naturally it is best to eat everything when it is still fresh.

STORAGE

1. Items will remain in a better state if kept in cool and dark surroundings. Root vegetables, especially potatoes should be kept in a dry paper sack, unscrubbed in a dark, dry place. Remember to keep the opening of the sack folded tightly down, otherwise they will sprout.
2. Tomatoes retain more flavour if they are kept out of the fridge.
3. Leafy greens, cauliflowers etc should remain in the crisper drawer of the fridge together with the salad vegetables.
4. Mushrooms lose a lot of moisture unless kept in paper bags in the fridge. It is best not to store them for too long as they do shrivel up.
5. Delicate vegetables e.g. asparagus are best eaten on the day of purchase.
6. Treat items with care as bruising will occur easily. If ever one item becomes over-ripe or damaged, remove it at once before it affects the rest of the batch.

PREPARATION

1. There is no need to peel vegetables. Much of the vitamin and mineral content lies just below the surface. This will be lost if the skin is removed. Therefore just give things a good wash, it is so much quicker and healthier.

2. Always use a sharp knife to cut vegetables, it causes less damage to those cells below the surface.
3. Remove tough stems from greens and cook the remaining leaf very briefy in a little fast boiling, salted water, with a tightly fitted lid for the pan.
4. DO NOT prepare vegetables a long time in advance, and leave them hanging around, or, even worse, soaking in water. Much of the goodness will be lost to the air or the soaking water as vitamins are volatile and evaporate rapidly.

COOKING METHODS

Boiling
Root vegetables go into cold water with a little salt, and a lid to cover.
   Green vegetables and new potatoes go into boiling salted water with a lid. This is a plain and simple way of presenting a whole range of vegetables. The cooking should only be until the vegetable is just cooked; it should still have a slight crunch to it.

Steaming
This is a good way of retaining flavour but it takes a little longer than boiling, even though the items are prepared in a smaller size. If you do not have a steamer, try putting the vegetables in a sieve over a pan of boiling water, cover with a lid. You could steam a selection of vegetables together provided they are of a similar size.

Baking
This is a good way of making full use of your oven space when making a meal. For example, potatoes cooked in vegetable stock. Washed potatoes are put in an ovenproof dish with enough stock to go half way up the potato, brush with melted butter and cook in a moderate oven until soft. All the stock should be absorbed by the potatoes. To serve, brush again with butter and sprinkle with parsley. No mess, no worry, it is easy and delicious. This method can be used with all root crops. If you do not want a browned top, as with turnips perhaps, cover the dish with foil or damp grease-proof paper.

Roasting
Providing not much fat is used, this is another nutritional way of cooking vegetables. There is the traditional roast spud, glazed chunks of turnip and swede and lovely parsnips roasted in honey.

Stir-Frying
Fine strips of vegetables are cooked briefly in very hot oil and served immediately. The time consuming bit is the chopping, but the effect is well worth it. Due to the quick cooking, the nutritional content remains quite high, and it certainly adds a new dimension to a meal.

First heat some oil in a large frying pan until a blue haze appears, this is a sign that the oil is really hot. The oil can be flavoured with a clove or garlic or a slice of root ginger but remove this before the vegetables are added. Stir the vegetables quickly in the oil for literally 2 minutes. They can be served at this stage. Alternatively, add some sauce made from a combination of the following: sherry, soy sauce (high in protein) or vegetable stock. (This is reduced a little whilst the vegetables are cooking). Because hardly any sauce is needed in the first place, 6 tablespoons is plenty for one pound (450 g) of vegetables. The sauce is well worth trying for the different effects it can give.

FOLLOWING THE SEASONS

'To everything there is a season' therefore it would be foolish to ignore it.

Although sophisticated growing methods, hot houses, refrigerated transport etc have extended the availability of many vegetables, no vegetable is ever as good as it is when it is in its natural season. Tomatoes eaten at the height of summer will have a far superior flavour to those grown in hot houses in the winter months; these might well have a superb colour, but the taste is sadly lacking.

What is the solution to this seasonal problem? Frozen or canned vegetables may well be very convenient but as with all processed foods much of the nutritional content is lost.

a) Freezing
    Vegetables are blanched or partially boiled; this stops enzyme

activity which could spoil and discolour the product during storage. Chemicals are added as with canning.

b) Canning.

Vegetables are frequently over-cooked during this process; salt and sugar are added together with chemicals used to produce bright colours.

The way to avoid additives is to freeze your own produce so you have control over what happens to the ingredients. But when all is said and done, by using vegetables in season your cooking will always taste better and be better for you. As the following tables show, there is plenty of choice.

SEASONAL VEGETABLE GUIDE

Spring	Summer		Autumn	Winter
Avocado	Avocado	Cucumber	Avocado	Jerusalem
Pear	Pear	Endive	Pear	artichoke
Artichoke	Tomatoes	Fennel	Beetroots	Beetroot
Beetroots	Artichokes	French beans	Broccoli	Broccoli
Broccoli	Asparagus	Lettuce	Cauliflower	Brussels
Cabbage	Aubergines	Mange tout	Celeriac	Sprouts
Carrots	Beetroots	Mushrooms	Fennel	Carrots
Mushrooms	Broad beans	Peas	Marrow	Celeriac
Spinach	Cabbage	New pota-	Mushrooms	Celery
Spring	Carrots	toes	Parsnips	Chicory
greens	Chillies	Radishes	Potatoes	Leeks
Oranges	Corn-on-Cob	Runner beans		Mushrooms
	Courgette	Spinach		Parsnips
		Spring greens		Potatoes
				Swede
				Turnips
				Watercress

Basic Root Vegetable Soup

1 medium onion – peeled, roughly chopped
1 medium potato – washed, cubed
1 medium swede – peeled, cubed
1 medium turnip – washed, cubed
1 medium parsnip – washed, cubed
2 medium carrots – washed, sliced
1 oz *(25 g)* butter or margarine
1 teaspoon dried mixed herbs
1 bay leaf
2 pts *(1.1 l)* vegetable stock

1 Try to cube the vegetables into a similar sort of size, this way they will cook evenly.

2 Melt the fat in a large saucepan, add the vegetables, cover and cook gently in the fat and the liquid that is produced during cooking (this process is known as sweating). Cook until the onion is transparent.

3 Add the herbs and vegetable stock, cover and simmer until the vegetables are completely soft. Season with salt and pepper.

This is the basic method for so many soups. Additions can be made at various stages for a slightly different end result.

a) Add a tablespoon of wholewheat flour before the stock is added. Cook the flour for a minute then add the stock. Continue to cook gently until the vegetables are soft. This obviously results in a slightly thickened soup.

b) A soup meal can be made by adding rice, pot barley or spaghetti to a basic vegetable soup. Add the rice or barley to the softened vegetables, turn in the oil and cook for a minute or so. Add the stock, cover and bring to the boil, then simmer until cooked. If using spaghetti, break the spaghetti into the bubbling liquid, reduce the heat, cover and simmer until cooked.

c) Add cooked pulses to the soup about 10 minutes before ready to serve to allow to heat through without breaking up.

d) Add half milk and half vegetable stock in more delicate soups like mushroom, watercress, lettuce, leek or cauliflower.

e) Add diced potatoes to the list of vegetables in a soup to be liquidised if you want a thicker end result without using flour.

Vegetable Gougere

Choux pastry:
3 ¾ oz *(95 g)* wholewheat flour
3 oz *(75 g)* butter or margarine
7½ fl oz *(225 ml)* water
a pinch of salt
2½–3 eggs – beaten
2 oz *(50 g)* cheese – cubed
1 teaspoon sage
freshly ground pepper

Vegetable filling:
1 medium onion – peeled, roughly chopped
½ green pepper – washed, deseeded, roughly sliced
½ red pepper – washed, deseeded, roughly sliced
1 small cauliflower – washed, divided into small florets
3 tomatoes – washed, roughly chopped
4 oz *(125 g)* mushrooms – wiped, roughly sliced

Sauce:
1½ oz *(40 g)* butter or margarine
1 oz *(25 g)* wholewheat flour
½ *(275 ml)* milk
2 teaspoons mixed herbs
salt and freshly ground pepper

Oven: 400°f, 200°c, G.M.6

1 Make the choux: In a saucepan, melt the fat in the water with the salt. When completely melted, bring to the boil. Once there are bubbles all over the surface, tip all the flour and sage in. Take off the heat and beat well with a wooden spoon. When everything is combined, put back on the heat and cook, stirring all the time, until the choux pastry begins to leave the sides of the pan clean (between 5–7 minutes). Remove from the heat and leave to cool.

All this happens very quickly so make sure the flour and sage are to hand so as not to ruin the final pastry.

2 Cook the vegetables: Soften the onion, pepper and small florets of cauliflower in 1½ oz (40g) of butter, cover and cook gently for 10 minutes until soft. Add the tomatoes and mushrooms and cook for a further 2 minutes.

3 Remove the vegetables, leaving the butter, add the flour to make the roux, cook for a minute. Remove from the heat and gradually add the milk. Put back on the heat and thicken, stirring all the time until it bubbles.

4 Put the vegetables in the sauce together with the herbs and season with salt and freshly ground pepper. Put to one side.

5 Finish the choux: Gradually beat in the beaten eggs to the choux mixture, give a really good mix in between each addition of egg. Add enough egg to make a smooth, shiny paste, which should be dropping consistency – you might not need all the egg. Stir in the cubed cheese.

6 Grease a flattish ovenproof dish – a quiche or pie dish for example, (the dish is served from its cooking container). Spoon the choux mixture around the edge of the dish and pile the filling into the middle of the ring.

Bake until the choux is well risen and brown and the filling is hot (35–40 minutes).

Vegetable Curry

2 onions – peeled, sliced
1 large parsnip – washed, roughly chopped
1 large swede – peeled, roughly chopped
1 large turnip – washed, roughly chopped
2 large carrots – washed, sliced
2 sticks celery – washed, sliced
4 courgettes – washed, sliced thickly
1 red pepper – washed, deseeded, sliced thickly
1 green pepper – washed, deseeded, sliced thickly
4 oz (125 g) mushrooms – wiped, sliced thickly
2 teaspoons curry powder – Madras or homemade
1 tablespoon tomato purée
2 tablespoons sultanas
1 cooking apple – washed, cored, roughly chopped
1 tablespoon Mango chutney
¼ pt (150 ml) vegetable stock
½ lemon – juice
salt and pepper to taste

1 Soften the root vegetables and the onion in a little oil in a large saucepan, cover and cook for 5–7 minutes.

2 Add the courgettes and peppers cook for a further 3 minutes.

3 Add the mushrooms and cook for a minute.

4 Add the curry powder, turn the vegetables in the spice and cook for a couple of minutes.

5 Add the sultanas, tomato purée, apple, mango chutney and vegetable stock. Simmer gently until the vegetables are cooked, 20–30 minutes. Season with salt and freshly ground pepper, add lemon juice to taste.

As with all curry dishes, they are best left a day before they are eaten, this gives the flavours a chance to develop and mingle.

Vegetable Puff

Any selection of vegetables is suitable, here is an example:

1 small aubergine – wipe, thinly sliced
salt
1 onion – peeled, roughly chopped
1 medium leek – washed, sliced
1 red pepper – washed. deseeded, sliced
1 green pepper – washed, deseeded, sliced
1 courgette – washed, sliced
6 tomatoes – washed, sliced (or a 15 oz (425 g) tin of tomatoes)

Topping:
8 oz *(225 g)* pot of Quark (or sieved cottage cheese, or Fromage frais)
4 oz *(125 g)* cheese – grated
2 eggs
¼ pt *(150 ml)* approx. milk
salt and pepper
wholewheat breadcrumbs – optional

Oven: 400°f, 200°c, G.M.6

1 Put the sliced aubergine into a bowl, put a good sprinkle of salt between each layer, (this is to remove the slightly bitter liquid of the aubergine). Leave for about 30 minutes. Drain the brown juice off, rinse under the cold tap to remove the salt, then squeeze dry.

2 In a saucepan with a small amount of oil, soften the onion, leek and peppers. When the onion is transparent, add the aubergine, courgette and tomato. Cover and cook until all the vegetables are cooked.

3 Make the puff: Mix together the Quark and eggs until smooth. Stir in the grated cheese, then add enough milk to make a thick pouring consistency, season with salt and pepper.

4 Put the vegetables into an ovenproof dish. Pour the topping on and spread evenly, sprinkle with breadcrumbs if used.

Bake for approximately 30 minutes until the top has puffed up and browned.

Courgette Lasagne

10 oz *(275 g)* wholewheat lasagne
1 onion – peeled, sliced
2 sticks celery – washed, sliced
1 green pepper – washed, deseeded, sliced
1 lb courgettes – washed, sliced
oil

Sauce:
2 oz *(50 g)* butter or margarine
1½ oz *(40 g)* wholewheat flour
1 pt *(575 ml)* milk
6 oz *(175 g)* flavoured hard cheese
e.g. Sage Derby, Cotswold (Double Gloucester with chives), Red Leicester – grated

Oven: 400°f, 200°c, G.M.6

1 Cook the lasagne: Bring a large saucepan of salted water with a tablespoon of oil to the boil. Add the sheets of lasagne one at a time to the bubbling water.

2 Once cooked, drain the pasta and run under the cold tap to stop the cooking (a process known as refreshing). Put to one side.

3 In a saucepan, soften the onion, celery and pepper. When the onion is transparent, add the courgettes. Cover and cook the vegetables until just soft, remove from the heat.

4 Make the cheese sauce: Melt the butter or margarine in a saucepan, once melted, add the flour and cook this roux for a minute, remove from the heat and stir in the milk. Return to the heat and bring to the boil, cook until the sauce thickens, for about 2 minutes.

5 Once thick, remove from the heat and stir in the cheese and season with salt and freshly ground pepper.

6 Grease a large deep ovenproof dish. Lay one-third of the pasta on the bottom, spoon a third of the vegetables over the top followed by some of the sauce.

7 Arrange another two layers of pasta, vegetables and sauce. Finish with a sauce layer.

Bake in the oven until golden brown, 30—35 minutes.

Vegetable Pizza

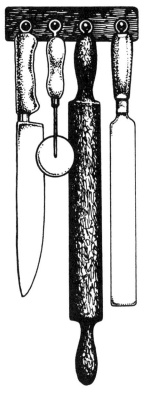

Bread dough:
½ oz *(15 g)* fresh yeast (or ¼ oz *(7 g)*
    dried yeast)
1 teaspoon sugar
¼ pt *(150 ml)* warm water
8 oz *(225 g)* wholewheat flour
1 teaspoon salt
1 teaspoon mixed herbs
5 tablespoons oil

Sauce:
1 large onion – peeled, roughly
    chopped
1 clove garlic – peeled, crushed
oil for cooking
3 tablespoons tomato purée
15 oz *(425 g)* tinned tomatoes
1 bay leaf
1 teaspoon salt
1 teaspoon oregano
1 teaspoon basil
1 teaspoon thyme

Decoration:
4 oz *(125 g)* mushrooms – wiped,
    sliced
rings of peppers – red, yellow, green
1–2 oz *(25–50 g)* cheese – grated
1 tablespoon pumpkin seeds

Oven: 425°f, 220°c, G.M.7

1 Make the bread base: Dissolve the sugar in about half the water,
   sprinkle the dried yeast over the top. Leave in a warm place for
   10 minutes to ferment.
   If using fresh yeast, cream the yeast and sugar together, add ½
   the warm water and leave in a warm place for 5 minutes to
   ferment.

2 Put the flour and salt in a bowl, make a dip in the centre, pour in
   the yeast mixture, add the rest of the liquid and the oil. Mix
   together into a soft ball. Knead to an elastic dough on a floured

surface, return to the bowl and leave to rise in a warm place for about an hour, either cover the bowl by a damp cloth or put it into a plastic bag.

3 Make the sauce: Soften the onion and garlic in a little oil in a saucepan, cook until transparent. Add the purée, tomatoes and herbs, and simmer gently until thick. Season with salt and pepper. The slower this can be done the richer the flavour.

4 Knock back the dough by kneading.(See Beginners Guide To Bread Making on page 177).

5 Form the pizza base: Place the dough on the floured surface, press into a circle with the flat of your hand. Pick up the dough, holding it by the edge. Move the dough around in a circle so it stretches down towards the table by its own weight, continue to move it around in this way until it has stretched to a circle with a diameter of 10 inches (25 cm).

6 Place the circle on a greased and floured baking tray or pizza plate if you have one.

7 Spread the by now thick tomato sauce over the surface, leave an inch border of bread showing.

8 Decorate with the sliced vegetables then the grated cheese followed by the pumpkin seeds.

Bake for 30 minutes until golden brown.

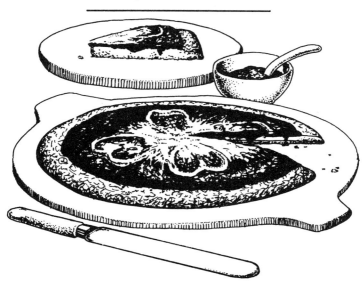

Leek and Tahini Crumble

1½ lbs *(700 g)* leeks – washed
8 oz *(225 g)* mushrooms – wiped
1 onion – peeled, roughly sliced
1 oz *(25 g)* butter or margarine
1 oz *(25 g)* potato flour (or
    wholewheat flour)
1 pt *(575 ml)* milk
1 teaspoon mixed herbs
salt and freshly ground pepper
1 tablespoon Tahini (sesame seed
    purée)

Crumble:
8 oz *(225 g)* wholewheat flour
4 oz *(125 g)* butter or margarine
1 tablespoon sesame seeds

Oven: 375°f, 190°c, G.M.5

1 Slice the leeks and the mushrooms, put into a saucepan with the onion and the fat, cover and sweat (soften in the fat and liquid produced during cooking) over a gentle heat.

2 Once the vegetables are soft and the onion transparent, add the flour, stir and cook for a minute.

3 Remove from the heat, gradually add the milk, mix well then return to a low heat to cook.

4 When the sauce has thickened, add the mixed herbs, season with salt and pepper. Add the Tahini, check the seasoning, then transfer to an ovenproof dish.

5 Make the crumble: Rub the fat into the flour until it resembles breadcrumbs. Sprinkle on top of the leek sauce. Scatter the sesame seeds on the top.

Bake for about 30 minutes, until the crumble is a rich nutty brown.

Dishes like this are an ideal way of using up bits of vegetables that you might have left over. If they are raw, soften them as at the beginning. Anything that has already been cooked, add to the sauce once it has thickened.

Savoury Rice Stuffed Peppers

4 large/8 small peppers (red or green)
4 oz *(125 g)* long grain brown rice
½ pt *(275 ml)* vegetable stock or water
    with Vecon or yeast extract
1 large onion – peeled, roughly
    chopped
1 clove garlic – peeled, crushed
oil
1 oz *(25 g)* almonds – unblanched,
    roughly chopped
4 oz *(125 g)* mushrooms – wiped,
    sliced
½ teaspoon oregano
1 teaspoon basil
3 tomatoes – washed, roughly
    chopped
1 tablespoon tomato purée
1 tablespoon sultanas
salt and freshly ground pepper
1 teaspoon mint sauce concentrate
    (or fresh mint – chopped)

Oven: 400°f, 200°c, G.M.6

1 Blanch the peppers: Cut the tops off as near to the top as possible, remove any seeds. Bring a saucepan of salted water to the boil. When it reaches a fast boil, put the peppers in, re-cover and cook for about 5 minutes until they soften a little.

2 Drain the peppers, hold under the cold tap until they cool, drain well (this process is known as refreshing).

3 Heat a small amount of oil in a saucepan, add the onion and garlic, cook for a few minutes then add the nuts, mushrooms and herbs, cook until the onion is transparent.

4 Add the rice, tomatoes, sultanas, purée and cook for a few minutes, stir well. Add the stock, season with salt and pepper and flavour with the mint sauce. Cover with a lid and cook until the rice is soft. Check the seasoning.

5 Place the peppers in a greased ovenproof dish. Fill with the rice stuffing. Cover with tin foil.

Bake for 30–40 minutes. When the peppers are soft, remove the foil, scatter the cheese on the top and return to the oven to brown.

This dish can also be cooked by using only the ring and the grill. Blanch the peppers for a little longer having made the filling first, keeping it hot. Drain the peppers and fill immediately. Put them into a dish, scatter the cheese over the top and brown off under a pre-heated grill.

Turkish Stuffed Aubergines

4 large aubergines
salt
2 large onions – peeled, roughly chopped
1 clove garlic – peeled, crushed
oil
15 oz (425 g) tinned tomatoes
½ teaspoon ground cinnamon
½ teaspoon cumin seeds – crushed (or use ground)
1½ oz (40 g) pine nuts
2 oz (50 g) raisins (or sultanas)
1 large lemon – squeezed

Oven: 350°f, 180°c, G.M.4
This is a quick way of preparing this spicy tomato and aubergine dish known as Iman Bayildi. It is really delicious and excellent eaten warm or cold, served with rice, for example, for a complete protein.

1 Wash the skins off the aubergines. Cut them in half, length-ways. Scoop out the pulp without piercing the skin. Leave a border of about ¼ inch (6mm) to act as a support.
2 Put the pulp into a bowl, sprinkle with plenty of salt between each layer sprinkle some salt inside the shells. The salt is used to bring out the slightly bitter aubergine juice (the process is called degorging). Leave to soak for at least 30 minutes.

3 After that time, rinse the salt off the pulp and shells under the cold tap. Turn the shells upside down to drain, squeeze the pulp to remove as much liquid as possible.

4 Make the tomato sauce: Soften the onion and garlic in a little oil. When the onion is transparent, add the spices and cook for a minute, add the tomato, pine nuts, raisins and aubergine, roughly chopped if a bit on the big side. Cook until the aubergine is soft.

5 Once soft and cooked, remove from the heat, season with salt and pepper, add the lemon juice to taste.

6 Snip some of the parsley heads off the stalks, leave some for the final decoration, stir into the sauce.

7 Arrange the aubergine shells in an ovenproof dish, divide the sauce between them, cover with tin foil or a lid.

Cook for an hour until the shells are soft. Serve warm or cold to get the full flavour of the dish.

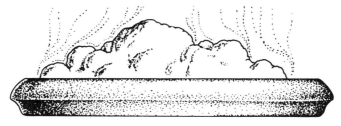

Spiced Cauliflower

1 medium cauliflower – washed, divided into florets
¼ pt *(150 ml)* mayonnaise
1 teaspoon clear honey
1 teaspoon white wine vinegar
1 teaspoon curry powder
1 teaspoon mango chutney
1 oz *(25 g)* mixed fruit and nuts

1 Bring some slightly salted water to a rapid boil. Cook the cauliflower for a few minutes in a covered pan, then drain.

2 Combine all the other ingredients together in a bowl then add the cauliflower, stir well, then chill to enable the flavours to mingle.

Vegetable Stuffed Buckwheat Pancakes with Quark

Pancake mix: makes 8 pancakes
1 oz *(25 g)* buckwheat flour
3 oz *(75 g)* wholewheat flour
a pinch of salt
1 egg
½ pt *(275 ml)* milk
oil for cooking

Filling:
1 medium leek – washed, finely
    sliced
½ red pepper – washed, deseeded,
    sliced
½ green pepper – washed, deseeded,
    sliced
½ yellow pepper – washed,
    deseeded, sliced
4 oz *(125 g)* mushrooms – wiped,
    sliced
4 oz *(125 g)* beansprouts
a knob of butter
1 teaspoon mixed herbs

Topping:
8 oz *(225 g)* pot of Quark (or Fromage
    frais, Petit Suisse)
milk
salt and freshly ground pepper

Oven: 375°f, 190°c, G.M.5

1 Make the batter: Put the flours and salt in a bowl, make a dip in the centre, break the egg into this and gradually add the milk. Whisk all the time to ensure a smooth paste.

2 The finished batter should be a pouring cream consistency. You might have to add a bit more milk. The batter should be left to stand at this stage to enable it to thicken; or it can be made well in advance.

3 Melt the knob of butter in a saucepan, add all the vegetables, cover and soften gently until they still have a slight crunch left. Add the mixed herbs, and put to one side.

4 Cook the pancakes: Heat some oil in a small frying pan. When the oil is hot (a blue haze will appear) pour off some of the oil into an ovenproof dish or strong bowl, leave about a teaspoon of oil in the pan.

5 Turn the heat down to moderate, add two tablespoons of the batter, swirling the pan around to give an even covering.

6 Once the batter is set, it will become a darker colour. Turn the pancake over with the help of a palette knife. The side that is now uppermost is the right side with its attractive lacy pattern. Cook the other side for 1–2 minutes.

7 Put the cooked pancakes on a plate as they cook, piling them up, keep in a warm place. After each pancake, reheat the pan with a teaspoon of oil before adding the next amount of batter.

8 When all the pancakes are cooked they can be filled with the softened vegetable filling.

With the lacy side of the pancake on the table, spoon some of the filling onto the pancake, roll it up and place in an ovenproof dish, repeat with the others.

9 Mix the Quark with enough milk (or skimmed milk) to make it the consistency of pouring cream. Season with salt and pepper. Pour over the pancakes.

Bake for 15–20 minutes until the top is golden brown.

Pancakes freeze very well. When they come out of the pan, inter-leave them with squares of greaseproof paper. When they are cold they can be wrapped or stored in a container and frozen. By inter-leaving the pancakes you will be able to defrost as many as you require rather than having to defrost the lot; it also makes separating easier.

Jacket 4 large baking potatoes
Potatoes

Oven: 400°f, 200°c, G.M.6

1 Scrub the potatoes well, then they are ready to cook. I always
stick a skewer through the potato lengthways as this helps them
to cook more quickly. It acts as a conductor, transferring the heat
through the dense mass of the potato. If you do not have
skewers, prick the skin of the potato with a fork, this will stop
them from bursting.

2 Put the potatoes straight onto the bars of the oven shelves so the
heat can circulate; if they are cooked on a baking tray you will
get soggy patches on the skin.

3 Cook for 1½–2 hours depending on their size. When cooked,
they should be soft to the touch with a crispy skin. The skin is
definitely the best bit, full of flavour and goodness and should
not be left on the plate at the end of the meal.

4 Once cooked, split the potatoes in half lengthways, or cut a cross
on one side and squeeze the skin to expose the soft flesh, serve
with butter or with a variety of fillings which can be simple or
exotic.

Filling ideas: (4 potatoes)

a) Soften a mixture of vegetables in some butter e.g. – peppers,
onion, mushrooms, tomatoes, sweetcorn, enough so there is
about a tablespoon per potato. Scoop out the flesh and mix with
these vegetables. Season with salt and pepper and herbs if
desired, pile the mixture back into the skins. Grate 4 oz (125 g)
of cheese, sprinkle over the potato halves and brown under a
hot grill until brown and bubbling.

b) Mix the potato flesh with butter, season with salt and pepper,
add 2 tablespoons of fresh parsley, mix in, then pile back into
the shells, top with sour cream (yoghurt, fromage frais or
cottage cheese) decorate with more parsley or perhaps a
sprinkling of paprika with some sesame seeds.

c) Scoop out the potato flesh, mix with 2 beaten eggs, salt and pepper, smooth this back into the shells, put sliced tomato over the cut surface, grate 4 oz (125 g) cheese, divide this between the potato halves, covering the tomato, put under a hot grill brown and bubble the cheese.

THE SALAD KIT

Vegetable	Fruit	Dressing	Miscellaneous
White cabbage	Apples	Yoghurt	Nuts
Red cabbage	Sultanas	Vinaigrette	Seeds
Tomatoes	Oranges	Mayonnaise	Cubed cheese
Cucumber	Pineapple	Sour cream	Cottage cheese
Celery	Grapes	Lemon juice	Dried shredded
Avocados	Bananas	Orange juice	coconut
Chicory	Strawberries	Vinaigrette	Cooked Pulses
Endive	Kiwi fruit	Piquant	Cooked rice
Lettuce	Melon balls	mayonnaise	Cooked whole-
Watercress	Grapefruit		grain wheat
Mustard & cress			Nut Loaf
Carrots			Strips of cold
Radish			omelette
Spring onions			Hard boiled
Fennel			eggs
Courgettes			Pâtés/dips
Cooked potatoes			Pasties
Mushrooms			Quiche
Cauliflower			Baked Beans
French beans –			Bread
blanched			Cooked pasta
Leeks – blanched			Bombay Mix
Peppers – red,			Tropical Mix
yellow, green			
Sweetcorn – cooked			
Cooked beetroot			
Sprouted seeds			
and pulses			

Fruit

There are many mouth-watering varieties of fruit available throughout the year in the shops. Thanks to improved storage and transportation, we can now enjoy luxuries from the other side of the world, even if the price is sometimes prohibitive to everyday consumption.

Fruit is a valuable source of natural sugars called fructose, glucose, and sucrose. These are easily used by the body as they are in a very pure form. Although the fruit contains a large amount of this type of sugar, it really is beneficial to the body because with it comes other valuable nutrients, minerals and vitamins. Fruit is therefore a necessary part of the diet and can be included in any meal in a variety of forms with tasty results.

DRIED FRUIT AND WHAT TO LOOK FOR

The best quality dried fruit is found in health food shops. It is sold loose and looks dull and sticky. The varieties sold in packets in supermarkets are not such a good buy, as they are coated in a mineral wax which is used to stop the fruit from sticking together . Although the fruit itself is not bad for you, it is advisable to wash the fruit before use if this is your only source, as this wax is considered to be harmful. Another addition to dried fruit is sulphur. It helps the lighter fruits such as peaches, pears, apricots, apples and sultanas, to dry and retains their pale and translucent appearance. Too much sulphur, however, puts a strain on the kidneys and prevents red blood cells from forming properly. Like all things, a little now and again will have no effect, but if you intend to include a regular amount of dried fruit in your diet, read the labels carefully, and make a point of going for the fruit sold loose with a rich dark colour. They will be more chewy, but the flavour will be far superior.

Storage

Even though the fruit is dried, this does not mean it will last in a first class condition for ever. It is best not to keep it for more than a month, because it has a tendancy to become tired looking and will taste very sugary. Have you ever eaten a handful of sultanas which have had large crystals of sugar in the middle? It is not very pleaasant. The answer is to keep small quantities in air-tight contaners, which will ensure a regular turnover of supplies. If by any chance you do come across old bits and pieces in the cupboard, there is no reason why they cannot be used in cooking; for puddings, cakes, biscuits, or soaked and then poached; this seems to bring them back to life and makes a quick, wonderful full-flavoured fruit compote. If eaten raw at this stage, the fruit might well taste gritty.

Fresh fruit should last well at room temperature but if kept too long, items will dry out. Apple skins begin to wrinkle and lose their juicy taste, citrus fruits become hard and dry, grapes take on a wine flavour then go brown and mouldy. So buy good quality fruit and eat it promptly.

Everyday Uses for Dried and Fresh Fruit
It is quite surprising how the addition of fruit to a dish can really lift and enhance the other ingredients. Fresh or dried fruit can be roughly chopped and added to salads, muesli, curries, sweet and sour dishes, risottos, made into sauce accompaniments, or used in breads, cakes, biscuits, soups. Much more should be made of fruit in the diet, it does not have to be restricted to sweet dishes in the traditional way. (The eating of fruit should be encouraged right from an early age, instead of awful junky snacks, sweets, and crisps eaten in ever increasing amounts between meals, fresh fruit would be a far more sensible alternative for all.)

Fruit, whether eaten fresh and raw, or dried and poached, when served with natural yoghurt does make the most delicious pudding. The colours are a feast for the eyes as the juice from the fruit combines with the white of the yoghurt. Damsons or blackcurrants served in this way are my all time favourites, the sight is gorgeous and it really does taste delicious. Fruit at breakfast is an invigorating way to start the day, half a grapefruit has made way for fresh fruit salads served with cereal and yoghurt or milk. Dried fruits cooked in a little honey with porridge is also a tasty combination.

Fruits combined with vegetables give salads a juicy-sweet taste. Watercress, orange and carrot salad tossed in an orange dressing, apple, celery and nut salad, potato, apple and sweetcorn salad are a few examples. Fruit can be added to the main course in dishes like curry as mentioned before or in the form of fruit chutneys which really do add a lovely bite to lentil dishes.

The more usual place for fruit is at the end of a meal, whether in the form of a big bowl of seasonal fruits on the table or served in the form of crumbles, pies, charlottes, mousses, fools, compotes, purées, sauces . . . and so the list goes on.

COOKING FRUIT

If you want to add a little extra sweetness when cooking fruit use either honey or raw sugar, that is to say anything but white sugar, which contains no goodness at all. Another way is to combine fresh and dried fruit together, apples and sultanas, apples and apricots.

There are several different methods of cooking fresh fruit as will be seen below, but to begin with dried fruit, the first step is the soaking:

a) *Soaking*
   As with anything that has been dried, before it can be used it must be reconstituted. You can choose from a variety of liquids, such as plain water, fruit juices such as orange or apple, perhaps with a dash of sherry or wine, or spirits and liquers for a special occasion. I think prunes are best soaked in tea. Strange as this may sound, this really does give the prunes the most wonderful sauce when cooked. Make a pot of tea in the normal way and just pour over the prunes until they are covered, leave to soak until they become plump then simmer gently. These days you can buy fruit teas which give some of the other fruits an interesting taste. Zest of lemon or orange can be added, and cinnamon sticks (quills) are a lovely addition to the lighter fruits like apricots.

b) *Cooking*
   When the fruit has soaked for at least three hours, it is cooked with the liquid over a low heat until it becomes soft and plump.

c) *Serving*
   Serve hot or cold with yoghurt, Fromage blanc (a soft creamy tasting 'cheese' made from skimmed milk, it tastes similar to yoghurt, but has a thicker consistency) or cream.

Poached Fresh Fruit

This is where the fresh fruit is cooked very gently, traditionally in a sugar syrup. The fruit becomes soft but still holds its shape.

Sugar Syrup:

1 pint (575 ml) of water, 10 oz (275 g) golden granulated sugar, lemon rind.

Dissolve the sugar in the water, bring to the boil and boil until it begins to feel tacky. Place the fruit in the syrup and simmer gently until cooked. This is usually between 5 and 10 minutes depending on the fruit.

This method, as you will see, requires rather a lot of sugar. The alternative is to use a couple of spoonfuls of honey, or to use straight orange juice or apple juice. This way you will end up with a lighter end result and will be able to taste the full flavour of the fruit. Lemon or orange zest, cinnamon sticks or whole cloves can be added to the syrup for extra depth of flavour.

Grilling Fresh Fruit

This is not a very usual way of serving fruit but it is quick and does make a lovely pudding. The first thing I remember cooking in this way was half a grapefruit sprinkled with sugar. Under the hot grill, the sugar caramelises to make a crunchy top; it does taste quite different like this.

With other fruits, lightly butter an ovenproof dish for a good flavour. Arrange the slices of unpeeled fruit in the dish, sprinkle with brown sugar and spice, or spoon over a little honey. This then goes under the grill where the fruit will soften slightly. The butter, natural fruit juices and sugar or honey will combine into a delicious sauce. Instead of slicing the fruit, leave in big chunks, thread on a skewer, brush with honey and grill. Serve with cream, yoghurt or perhaps a fresh fruit sauce, for example, apple kebabs with a purée made from stewed blackberries that have been sieved.

Baking Fresh Fruit

The example that springs instantly to mind is baked apples. Cooking apples are cored, put in an ovenproof dish with sultanas, a little sugar or honey, a knob of butter perhaps and spices. These are then baked until they are light and fluffy, the time taken will depend on the heat of the oven as this is the sort of dish that makes a good oven filler.

Whole pears can be baked in red wine served with cream or chocolate sauce for a simple but impressive looking pudding. Apricots and peaches can be cooked in the same way, using white wine. Fruit parcels are a fun way of presenting cooked fruit. Very roughly chop the fruit to be used, sprinkle with sugar or honey, mound into the middle of a square of tin foil, one per person, seal well, then bake. This works well for a barbeque.

NUTRITIONAL CONTENT

Vitamin C	Blackcurrants, redcurrants, citrus fruits, strawberries and gooseberries are good sources. High levels of the vitamin are only present in fresh fruit as cooking kills 50% and freezing 20% of this sensitive vitamin.
Vitamin K	This is not a very well known vitamin but it is needed for blood clotting. It is found in the pith of citrus fruits and their membrane. Therefore if preparing oranges, for example, just peel off the skin and pull the segments apart.
Carotene	This converts to vitamin A and is found in the yellow fruits like apricots, peaches, honeydew melons and mangoes.
Vitamin A	Blackcurrants, gooseberries, apricots and peaches contain good levels.
Thiamine (B_1)	All dried fruits with the exception of apricots and peaches are good sources. The best fresh sources are citrus, pineapples, melon, plums and bananas. The other B vitamins are found in small quantities in both dried and fresh fruits.

SEASONAL FRUIT GUIDE

Spring	Summer		Autumn	Winter
Bananas	Apricots	Limes	Bananas	Apples-
Mangoes	Bananas	Logan-	Blackberries	Eating
Pineapples	Bilberries	berries	Chinese	Cooking
Rhubarb	Black-	Mangoes	Goose-	Bananas
	currants	Melon	berries	Cranberries
	Cherries	Oranges	Figs	Grapefruit
	Damsons	Peaches	Grapes	Lemons
	Goose-	Pears	Limes	Limes
	berries	Pineapples	Melon	Lychees
	Grapes	Raspberries	Oranges	Manderines
	Greengages	Strawberries	Pears	Mangoes
			Pineapples	Oranges
			Pome-	Pineapples
			granates	Satsumas
			Satsumas	

Banana Cheese-cake

Base:
6 oz *(175 g)* Digestive biscuits (or plain homemade biscuits)
2 oz *(50 g)* butter or margarine
½ teaspoon ground ginger

Filling:
1 lemon – juice and zest
2 bananas
1 lb *(450 g)* curd cheese
3 tablespoons golden granulated sugar
¼ pt *(150 ml)* double cream

1 Put the biscuits into a plastic bag and roll over them with a rolling pin. Keep rolling until they are fine crumbs. Give the bag an occasional shake so you are not crushing the same bit all the time.

2 Melt the fat in a saucepan, add the ginger and the crumbs, and mix well.

3 Grease an 8″ (20cm) flan dish or quiche dish, (something you can serve the cheesecake from at the table to save the worry of having to turn it out, unless you have a loose bottom or spring clip tin).
Press the crumb mixture into the container, making an even layer by pressing down the crumbs with a jam jar or anything with a flat surface. Chill in the fridge while the filling is made.

4 Make the filling: Mash the bananas with a fork in a bowl, combine with the lemon juice and zest (remove the zest then squeeze the lemon, it is the easiest way).

5 Beat the cheese with the sugar. When soft, add the banana and lemon, mix until smooth.

6 Whip the cream until thick and smooth in texture, it should easily hold its shape. It is important to whip the cream to this stage otherwise the finished cheesecake will be on the runny side. The cream adds bulk and will thicken to a certain extent when it comes into contact with the lemon juice.

7 Gently fold the cream into the cheese mixture, pour on top of the base, cover to prevent colouration. Chill thoroughly for several hours or even overnight.

Once set the top can be decorated with slices of peeled Kiwi fruit, deseeded grapes, piped whipped cream, grated zest of lemon, chopped nuts or simply a good jam spread across the top.
Remember, slices of banana, if used for decoration will quickly turn brown unless liberally covered in lemon juice, so do this at the last minute. Remove any slices from left-over cheesecake for the same reason.

Spiced Apple Pudding

1½ lbs (700 g) cooking apples – washed, quartered, cored
2 oz (50 g) sultanas or raisins
½ teaspoon mixed spice
2 oz (50 g) Barbados sugar

Sponge:
4 oz (125 g) butter or margarine
4 oz (125 g) Barbados sugar
4 oz (125 g) self raising wholewheat flour
1 teaspoon mixed spice
2 eggs
milk
butter

Oven: 375°f, 190°c, G.M.5

1 Butter a pie dish. Roughly slice the apples into the dish. Sprinkle with sugar and mixed spice.

2 Make the sponge: Beat the fat and the sugar together until it becomes light and fluffy. Add the eggs one at a time with a little of the flour. When well combined, add the rest of the flour and the mixed spice. The sponge should be a dropping consistency – a little bit of milk might be needed to soften the mixture.

3 Spoon the sponge over the apples, smooth the surface.

Bake for 25–30 minutes until the sponge has well risen, evenly browned and is firm to the touch.

This pudding can be made with any fruit; rhubarb, blackberries, blackcurrants, or even with a combination of fresh and dried fruits, sultanas, apricots, peaches or apple rings for example.

Baked Pears in Orange Juice with Cinnamon

4 large Comice pears
orange juice
½ teaspoon ground cinnamon (or 1 cinnamon quill)

Oven: 350°f, 180°c, G.M.4

1 Wash the pears. Using a potato peeler, sections of the skin can be removed to make a pattern, otherwise just put the pears straight into an ovenproof dish or casserole.
2 Pour in enough orange juice to go half way up the pears, add the cinnamon.
3 Cover with tin foil and bake for 10–15 minutes until the fruit is just soft. The blade of a knife or a skewer should pass easily into the flesh.

Serve warm with the poaching liquid and cream, yoghurt or chocolate sauce.

Chocolate sauce:
4 oz (125 g) carob chocolate bar (orange flavour perhaps)
3 fl oz (100 ml) water (or orange juice)
1½ oz (40 g) unsalted butter

Put all the ingredients into a bowl, place this over a saucepan of gently bubbling water. Melt the ingredients, stir occasionally. Before serving remove from the heat and beat well. Serve warm with the warm pears.

Fluffy Apricot Pie

Pastry:
6 oz *(175 g)* wholewheat flour
3 oz *(75 g)* butter or margarine
a pinch of salt
2–3 tablespoons water

Filling:
2 eggs
1 egg yolk
5 oz *(150 g)* golden granulated sugar
4 oz *(125 g)* butter – melted
¼ pt *(150 ml)* natural yoghurt
4 oz *(125 g)* dried apricots – soaked
  overnight

Oven: 400°f, 200°c, G.M.6

1 Gently cook the apricots in their soaking water in a saucepan over a low heat for about 15 minutes until they are soft. Remove once cooked and cool.

2 Make the pastry: Rub the fat into the flour until it resembles fine breadcrumbs, add the salt and enough water to bring the ingredients together into a soft ball.

3 On a lightly floured surface, with a floured rolling pin, roll out the pastry into a circle big enough to line a 8–9″ (20–22 cm) flan tin. Press down well, trim away the unwanted pastry around the edge.

4 Bake the pastry case blind: Cover the case with a sheet of greaseproof paper, weigh this down with some dried pulses or a· pad of tin foil.

5 Bake for 10–15 minutes. Remove from the oven.
Turn the oven down to 350°f, 180°c, G.M.4

6 Remove the paper from the flan ring. Keep the beans separately from your other ones, now they can only be used for baking blind.

7 Make the filling: Whisk the eggs, egg yolk and sugar until fluffy, at the same time, melt the butter gently.

8 Add the butter and the yoghurt to the egg mix, whisk well until everything is combined.

9 Roughly chop the cooked apricots and fold into the egg mix, pour into the pastry case.

Bake for 30–35 minutes until the filling is set and golden brown.

Fruity Jam Sponge Tart

Pastry:
6 oz *(175 g)* wholewheat flour
3 oz *(75 g)* butter or margarine
a pinch of salt
2–3 tablespoons water

Filling:
4 good tablespoons of Whole Earth jam

Sponge:
4 oz *(125 g)* butter or margarine
4 oz *(125 g)* Barbados sugar
4 oz *(125 g)* wholewheat self raising flour (add 1 teaspoon of baking powder if using plain)
2 eggs

Decoration:
1 oz *(25 g)* flaked almonds

Oven: 375°f, 190°c, G.M.5

The pastry base with the light sponge on the top makes a simple and attractive pudding for any day of the week.

1 Make the pastry: Rub the fat into the flour and salt until it resembles fine breadcrumbs, add the salt and enough water to bring the ingredients together into a soft ball.

2 On a lightly floured surface with a floured rolling pin, roll out the pastry in a circle big enough to line an 8″ (20 cm) flan tin. Press down well. Trim away any overhanging pastry from the edge with a knife. Prick the bottom with a fork all over.

3 Spoon the jam over the bottom of the pastry case making an even layer.

4 Make the sponge: Beat the fat and the sugar into a bowl until light and fluffy. Add the eggs one by one with a couple of spoonfuls of flour, mix well. Add the rest of the flour and beat for a few minutes, a dropping consistency is required, so add enough water until the mixture will just slip off a spoon.

5 Spread the sponge on top of the jam, smooth the surface, sprinkle the top with the flaked almonds.

Bake for 30 minutes until an even brown. Check to see if the sponge is cooked by placing your hand on the top, the sponge should feel set and springy.

Quick Date and Walnut Cake

4 oz *(125 g)* golden granulated sugar
¼ pt *(150 ml)* water
8 oz *(225 g)* dried dates
2 oz *(50 g)* walnuts – roughly chopped, keep 3 good bits for decoration
3 oz *(75 g)* butter or margarine
4 oz *(125 g)* wholewheat self raising flour
a pinch of bicarbonate of soda

Oven: 325°f, 170°c, G.M.3

Grease a 1½ lb loaf tin.

1 Put the sugar, water, dates, walnuts and fat into a saucepan, and melt gently over a low heat. Break the dates up a bit with a wooden spoon this will help them to soften.

2 Once the fat has melted and the dates are soft, remove from the heat, add the flour and the bicarbonate of soda, arrange the reserved pieces of walnut on the top.

Cook for about 45 minutes. After 30 minutes, check the cake, put a knife into the centre of the cake. If the knife should come out clean the cake is done.

Date and Orange Fingers

12 oz *(350 g)* **dried dates**
6 tablespoons orange juice
zest of an orange
6 oz *(175 g)* **wholewheat flour**
6 oz *(175 g)* **jumbo oats**
3 oz *(75 g)* **Barbados sugar**
5 oz *(150 g)* **margarine or butter**

Oven: 400°f, 200°c, G.M.6

1 Gently heat the dates, orange zest and juice (squeeze the orange used for the zest, then make up the liquid with the juice from a carton) until the dates are soft. Break them up with a wooden spoon once in the saucepan.

2 In another saucepan melt the fat and the sugar. Once melted, stir in the flour and oats. Mix well to make sure everything is well covered in the fat.

3 Grease a baking tin 11" x 7" (27 x 18cm) press half the oat mixture over the bottom of the tin. Make sure you press it down well so it will stick firmly together, this is best done with your hand to get an even layer.

4 Spread the date mixture evenly over the top. Sprinkle the remaining oat mixture over the top, press down firmly again.

Bake for 20 minutes. Cool in the tin for a few minutes, carefully mark the 16 fingers then leave to cool completely before trying to remove the fingers from the tin.

Quick Fruit Scone Round

8 oz *(225 g)* **self raising wholewheat flour (add 2 teaspoons of baking powder if using plain)**
3 oz *(75 g)* **butter or margarine**
1 oz *(25 g)* **Barbados sugar**
3 oz *(75 g)* **sultanas**
7 tablespoons milk (or half milk and water)

Oven: 425°f, 220°c, G.M.7

1 Rub the fat into the flour (and baking powder if used) until it resembles fine breadcrumbs. Stir in the sugar and sultanas. Add enough of the milk to make a soft but not wet dough, making sure all the flour is incorporated.

2 On a lightly floured surface, tip out the dough. Gently press it into a circle 1" (4½ cm) thick.

3 Put the dough onto a greased baking sheet, mark 8 sections with a knife.

Bake for 10–15 minutes until golden brown.

Once cooked, cool on a wire rack. The scones are best eaten on the same day.

Orange Shortbread

9 oz (250 g) wholewheat flour
6 oz (175 g) butter or margarine
3 oz (75 g) golden granulated sugar
1 orange – zest

Oven: 300°f, 150°c, G.M.2

1 Rub the fat into the flour until it resembles fine breadcrumbs, stir in the sugar and the orange zest.

2 Bring the ingredients together into a soft ball, knead gently in the bowl.

3 Either roll out on a lightly floured surface into a circle and place on a greased baking sheet, or smooth into a baking sheet about 7 x 9" (18 x 23 cm).

4 Prick the surface with a fork.
Bake for about 45 minutes or until the shortbread feels firm on the surface.

5 Divide up as soon as it comes out of the oven and leave to cool slightly in the tin. Finish the cooling on a wire rack.

Sultana Tea Bread

8 oz *(225 g)* **sultanas**
8 oz *(225 g)* **raisins**
½ pt *(275 ml)* **strong tea**
6 oz *(175 g)* **Barbados sugar**
6 oz *(175 g)* **butter or margarine**
12 oz *(350 g)* **wholewheat flour**
1 **large egg**

Oven: 300°f, 150°c, G.M.3

Grease a 9 x 6" (23 x 15 cm) baking tin.

1 Make the tea with boiling water, leave to brew for a few minutes. Strain the tea into a saucepan and add the fruit. Gently simmer the fruit for 6–8 minutes until it becomes plump. As an alternative the fruit can be soaked overnight.

2 Once the fruit is done, add the fat and sugar, melt over a low heat, stir occasionally so the sugar dissolves and does not stick to the bottom.

3 Once the fat has melted, remove from the heat, add the flour and stir well then add the egg making sure all the ingredients are well combined.

4 Put the mixture into the prepared tin, smooth the top.

Bake for 1½ hours. Check after an hour by placing a knife or skewer into the centre, if it comes out clean the cake is done.

Best eaten warm with butter.

Orange and Chocolate Cake

8 oz *(225 g)* **butter or margarine**
8 oz *(225 g)* **Barbados sugar**
8 oz *(225 g)* **wholewheat flour**
2 teaspoons baking powder
1 oz *(25 g)* Carob powder
5 eggs
1 orange – zest

Oven: 300°f, 150°c, G.M.2

Grease an 8" (20 cm) cake tin.

1 Put the fat, sugar and zest into a bowl and beat until soft and paler in colour. If the ingredients are well creamed at this stage, the cake will have a good light texture.

2 Add the eggs one at a time with a little of the flour and carob powder. Mix well between each addition.

3 Add the rest of the flour, carob powder and the baking powder, again make sure everything is well mixed by scraping down the sides of the bowl at regular intervals.

4 Put the mixture into the cake tin, and smooth over the top.

Bake in the middle of the oven for 1¼ hours. Check after 45 minutes, turn the cake around on the shelf half way through the cooking time so that it cooks evenly. To check if it is cooked, place a skewer or knife into the centre, if it comes out clean the cake is cooked.

Turn out onto a wire rack, leave to cool.

To make this cake even more delicious top it with a melted chocolate icing:

2 bars orange carob chocolate
3 tablespoons orange juice
1 oz (25g) butter

Put all the ingredients in a bowl (not plastic) over a saucepan of gently bubbling water. Stir occasionally. Once melted, beat until smooth, pour over the cake quickly, smooth with a warm knife (leave it to stand in warm water for a while).

Dairy Products

The thought of dairy products conjures up images of scrubbed parlours with churns of milk, wooden butter makers, huge bowls of cream and truckles of cheese, covered in cloth, maturing on slatted shelves in a nearby cellar – somewhat unrealistic in today's world of the modern technological, high production dairies, with their sterile rooms and huge stainless steel equipment. Fed by a continual stream of tanker lorries arriving every day from all over the county, they satisfy customer demand for milk, butter, creams, cheese and yoghurt.

Dairy products are used by nearly everyone as part of their diet in some form or another. They do contain animal fats which are high in cholesterol but, provided they are eaten in moderation, in conjunction with a varied wholefood diet, they provide an extremely nutritious, convenient food source. Milk is not just a drink, but a balanced food in its own right, providing ⅓rd the daily protein allowance, this will also apply to its by-products too.

MILK

Milk is thankfully plentiful and has remained relatively cheap. It is packed full of calcium and other nutrients such as potassium and phosphorus, together with vitamins A and B, thiamine and riboflavin. Milk undergoes several different processes which produce slightly different end results:-

Types of Milk
a) Raw milk – comes straight from the cow and is therefore untreated. It is difficult to obtain as, all milk for retail sale has to be heat treated to kill off potentially harmful bacteria.
b) Pasteurised milk – is the type most readily available. Its bottle has a silver top. The milk is rapidly heated then quickly cooled to kill any bacteria, which does slightly affect the vitamin content.
c) Homogenised milk – This is heat treated as pasteurised, then processed in such a way that breaks down the globules of fat already in the milk. This way they remain evenly distributed

throughout the liquid rather than rising to the top as 'cream'; hence the creamy-tasting 'top of the milk' in pasteurised milk. The bottle top is red.

d) Gold top milk – This has a high cream content and comes solely from Jersey, Guernsey or South Devon cows. Because of the high levels of fat, the milk is rich and creamy tasting.

e) U.H.T. – This is homogenised milk that has been Ultra Heat Treated to a temperature of 135°–150°c (275°–300°f). This process imparts long life properties, enabling it to be stored for up to six months. Once opened, use as fresh i.e. keep in the fridge, and use within two days.

f) Skimmed milk – This has had enough 'cream' skimmed off during processing to leave a fat content of not more than 0.3%.

g) Low fat skimmed – This is made from skimmed milk which has been spray dried in a current of hot air, or passed between heated rollers. The result is the removal of water, leaving a powder containing only milk solids. Add warm or cold water to reconstitute, and use as for normal milk.

Evaporated and condensed milk products are highly processed and should not be included in the diet.

Goat's milk

This is becoming more readily available these days, being sold straight from local goat owners or from health shops, but it hasn't quite reached the supermarkets yet.

It has a major advantage in that unlike other milk, it can be frozen. This is due to an even distribution of fat. Its easy storage might be a factor to make you think twice about trying it.

Goat's milk is often used as an alternative for children who show allergies to cow's milk. The fat distribution makes it easier for them to digest as it is similar in character to human milk.

Soya Milk

This is a 'milk' produced from soya flour and so is therefore a valuable food for vegans.

Nutritional Content

Calcium, potassium, phosphorus and vitamins A, B and D are available in milk and from a variety of other food sources, so it is not actually essential to drink vast quantities each day. If you look at the complete protein diagrams, you will see, milk is used in conjunction with other food groups will give you far more in the way of vital elements and fibre, than always drinking it on its own.

Uses of milk

Many savoury sauces stem from the basic 'white' or bechamel sauce. Here, melted butter and flour are cooked together to form a roux or paste. Milk that has been infused with herbs and onion over a gentle heat, is then strained and added. The sauce is stirred over a gentle heat until it boils and thickens.

This 'mother' sauce can then be flavoured with sautéed onions, mushrooms, cheese, herbs or hard boiled eggs and served in a variety of ways, as a topping for vegetables, with pasta or pulse dishes and savoury pancakes. Milk is also used in baking for cakes, biscuits, scones and puddings.

Yoghurt

Yoghurt comes in all shapes and sizes these days: Low fat, full fat, whole milk, skimmed milk, natural, flavoured, French style, Greek style. But, when all is said and done, they are all made of milk.

Yoghurt was made by the Balkans originally, and has only recently gained such acclaim in the West, where we are beginning to appreciate its full potential. It is a simple food, which can easily be made at home. Milk has harmless bacteria (Lactobacillus bulgaricus and Streptococcus thermophilus) introduced to it, then by keeping the liquid warm, the organisms will feed on the milk sugars, gradually producing slight acidity, which eventually sets the milk proteins.

The result is a thick, set, tangy, creamy white, smooth textured product, equal in food value to milk, with easy to digest properties. Yoghurt is of benefit to health as the bacteria present remains in the digestive system, where it helps with the break down of other foods, restoring the natural balance in the body, especially if there are any digestive problems or if antibiotics have been prescribed (these tend to kill off useful bacteria in the intestine).

When a carton says 'live' yoghurt it means the Lactobacillus is still alive; this is extremely beneficial to the body as the yoghurt is a 'living' and therefore very active product, full of health giving properties and is the best sort of yoghurt to use as a 'starter' when making a yoghurt at home.

Uses of yoghurt
1. Eaten on its own as a pudding, or with fruit, fresh or cooked, topped with sesame seeds or nuts.
2. Used as a substitute for cream as a topping or in mousses etc.
3. Used in baking in cakes and scones.
4. Used as a salad dressing flavoured with herbs, black pepper or crushed garlic. To make it thicker, add 2 tablespoons of oil to ¼ pint of yoghurt.
5. Adding yoghurt in equal quantities with mayonnaise produces a lighter texture and flavour.
6. It is easy to make cheese from yoghurt. Pour yoghurt into some cheesecloth or clean linen, tie and hang over a bowl to drip. The light cheese that is produced is commercially sold as Quark.

Cream
Sour, single, whipping, double and clotted cream have increasing percentages of fat. That is, the thicker they are, the more fat they contain, and because of this, they really should be used sparingly. If you do like a little cream (once in a while!) why not try sour cream for a change. It has a thick, smooth creamy texture with a light flavour, not at all sour as might be expected.

BUTTER

Butter is made from the churning of cow's milk. The creamy fat globules coagulate during the agitation to form 80% butter fat. This is then pressed together to extract the water. Salt is added if required before packaging. The final flavour and colour will depend on whether salt is added or not, salt gives the rich yellow colour and pronounced taste whereas unsalted is pale with a totally different sort of flavour. Butter is the best fat to use in cooking, especially for cakes and pastries because of its wonderful flavour, or just dabbed onto vegetables or spread on bread. It is however expensive and very high in cholesterol. An alternative might well be margarine.

Margarine
This was invented by a French chemist who had been ordered by Napolean III to find an alternative for butter.
    Present day margarine is made from a variety of vegetable oils,

which are sometimes mixed with animal or fish fats. These are hydrogenated to form a solid fat which is then churned with milk, salt and vitamins. Always read the label to check just what has gone into the product. Pure vegetable margarines include names like Granose, Nutter, Trex and Tomor. Nutter, for example, contains a carefully balanced mixture of nut oils and Tomor is a pure blend of vegetable oils and so is especially suitable for vegans. All the vegetable margarines are best used straight from the fridge.

Soft margarines/table margarines.
Some of these have a small amount of butter in them to improve the flavour, but the majority are made entirely of vegetable oils which as you now know, are high in polyunsaturated fats. They are only suitable for spreading and if heated they would burn very easily.

CHEESE

All cheeses are based on milk of some kind or another. This is churned with rennet (this is a substance extracted from the stomachs of calves which enables milk to curdle. Now there is a vegetable alternative available). Once the milk has curdled, curds and whey are produced. The curds (the solids) are removed totally or partially from the whey (the clear liquid) by either heating or pressing or both. It is then matured and turned regularly.

Cheese is one of the oldest forms of food known to man. The Romans were cheesemakers and encouraged its production wherever their Empire spread. Over the years, cheese has developed into many different types and varieties as man has devised ways of making it with different consistencies and flavours. So you will never be bored and it is so versatile. Eaten hot, cold, on its own or as part of other dishes, it is an excellent and convenient food.

Food value
Cheese holds as much protein weight for weight as prime beef for a fraction of the price. As it is milk based, it is packed with calcium, vitamins A, D and B_2 and the quantities of fat are needed for keeping warm, good skin and glossy hair.

What to look for in a whole cheese.
1. A hard or semi-hard cheese such as cheddar should be firm, even slightly flaky or crumbly.
2. The outer skin should not be cracked.
3. The outer layer should not have tiny beads of fat on the cut surface, or look sweaty. This shows it has been stored, or uncovered in too warm a temperature.
4. Cheese should be more or less the same colour throughout.
5. A dark colour near the rind shows the cheese is old and dry.
6. Any blue sheen or white specks indicate mould and a musty flavour.
7. Taste a cheese if you can before purchase, even a strong cheese should not be harsh or acid tasting.
8. The milder, softer semi-hard cheese such as Edam (in the red wax coating) should be velvety when cut, not moist and flaky and should have the same creamy colour all the way through. There should be a definite cheese taste not a 'soapy' one.

Buying Cheese
Whenever possible, buy your cheese freshly cut from a large block, this way you will be buying a better quality product with a far superior taste to the vaccumed packed types which do not have the chance to mature properly.
1. Always look for a top quality cheese to avoid disappointment. If you thought you wanted Cheddar but the Cheshire looks better, have it. A low quality product tastes less pleasant, spoils easily when cooked and does not store as well.
2. By buying off a block of cheese, free from wrappings, you will easily be able to assess its texture and condition, and you can ask to taste it. Even the same type and grades of cheese can vary a lot in flavour.
3. If a Camembert or Brie (soft ripening cheese) is already running out from under the crust in the shop, it will spoil very quickly at home. On the other hand, if you try to eat it while it is under ripe, the taste will also be disappointing.
4. Blue cheese should be evenly coloured without greyish patches, the blue veins being definite in contrast with the creamy coloured cheese. It should look crumbly and moist, the flavour is strong with a tendency to become harsh with age.

Storing Cheese

1. A small piece will not keep as well as a larger slab as it will dry out quickly.
2. Cheese does not go bad or become unfit to eat if stored for a long period of time. The food value will stay the same, but the texture and flavour might be affected.
3. If you do not have a covered cheese dish or a cool larder, the answer is the fridge. Keep cheese tightly wrapped in foil in the least coldest part. To serve, remove and unwrap at least two hours before required, to allow the chill to disappear.
4. Cheese stored in the fridge will last for 2 weeks if hard or semi-hard and 1 week if soft or semi-soft before it is past its best.
5. Do not freeze it unless absolutely necessary as it becomes grainy and easily crumbled. At this stage it is only suitable for cooking.

Cheese Categories

1. Hard: – e.g. Cheddar and Double Gloucester. Look out for ones made with vegetable rennet, available in health shops.
2. Semi-hard: – e.g. Edam and Gouda – sold in red and yellow wax coverings respectively. Fairly mild cheeses with slightly fewer calories than hard cheeses.
3. Veined: – e.g.Stilton and Danish Blue. The cheese have thin wires drawn through them, the air and naturally present bacteria get to work to produce the blue colouration or mould.
4. Soft ripening: – e.g. Brie, Camembert. Tasty soft cheeses encased in a white crust, they should be soft and nicely matured before eating.
5. Curd is the soft smooth cheese made when milk is allowed to turn naturally. Commercially, it is more likely to be made by the addition of a lactic starter. This separates the curd and whey in the milk, the curds being sold as cheese.
6. Cream is made in a similar way to curd only cream is used instead of milk.
7. Cottage cheese is a type of curd cheese made from skimmed milk with the addition of rennet. The resulting curds are cut and washed to produce the familiar granular appearance.

EGGS

Eggs are one of the most versatile of ingredients in the kitchen. They can be included in sweet or savoury dishes or used by themselves in the form of boiled, poached, scrambled, baked or fried eggs – each example having a distinctive flavour and texture. Eggs are good meal stretchers and provide a convenience food that can produce a satisfying meal in minutes.

Nutrition

One egg will supply 1/10th of the average daily protein requirement for an adult, containing about 80 calories. As they are digested slowly, they are good for dieters.

They contain vitamins A, D, thiamine, riboflavin, B_{12}, biotin and vitamin E. Minerals include iron, calcium, potassium, magnesium, and folic acid which is 50% higher in a free range egg than a battery egg, an important consideration for vegetarians as no other food contains this in such high quantities.

Types of eggs

Avoid battery or deep litter eggs as the chickens have not led a very natural life. They never see the light of day, and are fed on chemically treated grain, which can not be good for them. Free range is by far the best; the birds are far healthier as they are allowed to grub around outside, and a happy bird must result in better quality eggs with deep coloured yolks and good whites.

The fresh egg test.

Place the egg (still in its shell) in a jug of water.

a) If it stays on its side at the bottom it is fresh.

b) If it rises slightly at either end, it isn't quite as fresh.

c) If it floats or stands upright, it really is stale and should be thrown away. This is due to the naturally present air sack gradually getting bigger as the egg gets older.

A cracked fresh egg will have a high, round yolk, surrounded by a thick circle of white encircled by a thinner ring of white.

A stale cracked egg will have a flattish yolk with a thin runny white.

Cheese Soup

1 medium onion – peeled, roughly chopped
1 medium potato – washed, roughly chopped
1 medium leek – washed, slice the white part only (keep the green for your next batch of veg. stock)
1 clove garlic – peeled, crushed
1 tablespoon oil
½ teaspoon sage
½ teaspoon thyme
bay leaf
1 pt (575ml) vegetable stock
½ pt (275 ml) milk
6 oz (175 g) Cheddar cheese – grated
sea salt and freshly ground pepper to taste

1 Soften the vegetables in a little oil in a covered saucepan without burning, over a low heat, until the onion is transparent.

2 Add the vegetable stock and herbs, bring to the boil covered, then simmer until the vegetables are completely cooked.

3 Add the milk and simmer for a few minutes.

4 Liquidise the soup – whizz a small amount at a time, so it does not leak out of the top. By doing it in small amounts you can ensure a smooth uniform texture to the final soup.

5 Return to the heat, add the grated cheese, stir in over a low heat. Do not let this boil as that will make the cheese go stringy.

Check the seasoning and adjust with sea salt and the freshly ground pepper.

Savoury Cheese-cake with Mush-rooms

Pastry:
8 oz *(225 g)* wholewheat flour
4 oz *(125 g)* butter or margarine
a pinch of salt
3–4 tablespoons water

Filling:
1½ oz *(40 g)* butter or margarine
6 oz *(175 g)* button mushrooms –
    wiped, sliced
2 tablespoons plain wholewheat
    flour
¼ pt *(150 ml)* milk
2 teaspoons French mustard
10 oz *(275 g)* curd cheese (or sieved
    cottage cheese)
3 eggs – separated
salt and freshly ground pepper

Decoration:
3 tomatoes – washed, sliced
1 oz *(25 g)* cheese – grated
reserved cooked mushrooms

Oven: 350°f, 180°c, G.M.4

1 Make the pastry: Rub the fat into the flour and salt until it resembles breadcrumbs. Add enough water to make a soft dough, bringing all the ingredients together in a ball.

2 On a floured surface, roll the pastry out into a circle.

3 Grease an 8–10" (20–25 cm) deep cake tin with a loose bottom. Slip the pastry into the tin, press firmly to the bottom, right up to the edge. Work up the sides of the tin. There should be a lip of at least an inch, it does not have to be even as long as there is enough to support the filling. Prick the pastry with a fork.

4 Bake blind: Cover the pastry with greaseproof paper held down by a snugly fitting pad of foil or by dried pulses. This will stop the pastry case from rising during cooking as the weight prevents air bubbles which would spoil the finished case.

5 Cook the case for 10 minutes, remove from the oven, carefully

remove the paper and its weight. These can be used again.

6 Make the filling: Melt the butter in a saucepan, add the mushrooms, cook for a few minutes, remove a couple of tablespoons once soft, put to one side and keep for decoration. Stir in the flour and cook for a minute. Gradually add the milk, stir well until the sauce thickens, remove from the heat.

7 In a large bowl, beat the curd cheese, egg yolks and mustard. When smooth stir in the mushroom sauce and season with salt and pepper.

8 Whisk the egg whites until they are smooth and the same consistency as the mushroom sauce. If the whites are overwhipped they will not combine very evenly with the other ingredients.

9 Gently fold the egg whites into the sauce using a figure of eight movement so as not to knock too much of the air out.

10 Spoon the mixture into the cooked pastry case. Arrange the cooked mushrooms on the top, together with the sliced tomatoes. Sprinkle with the grated cheese.

Bake until golden brown and set for 35–45 minutes. Leave to cool for a few minutes, then carefully free the sides and remove from the tin when cold.

Egg and Onion Layer

2 large onions – peeled, thinly sliced
1 medium leek – washed, thinly sliced
4 oz (125 g) mushrooms – wiped, thickly sliced
4 oz (125 g) butter or margarine
2 tablespoons oil
1 teaspoon mixed herbs
10 oz (275 g) wholewheat breadcrumbs
4 oz (125 g) cheese – grated
6 eggs

Sauce:
1 oz *(25 g)* **butter or margarine**
1 oz *(25 g)* **wholewheat flour**
½ pt *(275 ml)* **milk**
1 teaspoon mixed herbs
1 teaspoon mustard

Oven: 350°f, 180°c, G.M.4

1 Put the eggs into a saucepan of cold water, cover and bring to the boil, reduce the heat and simmer for 10 minutes. Drain the water off the eggs and run under the cold tap until the eggs are cold, leave the eggs sitting in the saucepan of cold water until they are needed. This cooling process is to stop the grey ring that sometimes occurs between the yolk and the white of a hard boiled egg.

2 Heat a tablespoon of oil in a frying pan. Cook the onion and leeks until the onion begins to soften, add the mushrooms and continue to cook until the onion is transparent.

3 Once cooked, remove the vegetables from the pan, put to one side. Heat the rest of the oil together with the margarine or butter. Once melted, add the breadcrumbs and fry until golden brown and crunchy. Stir regularly to avoid burning. Add the mixed herbs towards the end of cooking. Once browned, remove from the heat, allow to cool for a few minutes then stir in the grated cheese.

4 Make the sauce: In a saucepan melt the 1 oz (25 g) of fat, add the flour and cook for a minute to make the roux. Remove from the heat and gradually add the milk mixing well. Return to the heat and stir until it thickens. Season with salt, pepper, mustard and mixed herbs.

5 Crack and peel the eggs. Slice lengthways.

6 Assemble the dish: Place half the fried breadcrumb mixture on the bottom of a casserole or pie dish. Put half the vegetables on the top of this. Spoon over a little of the sauce, lay the eggs on the top of the sauce, with the rest of the vegetables on the top followed by the remaining sauce and top with the rest of the breadcrumb mix.

Bake for 20 minutes to warm through.

Curried Eggs

Sauce:
1 large onion – peeled, roughly
  chopped
oil
1 medium cooking apple – washed,
  cored, roughly chopped
1 dessertspoon curry powder
1 tablespoon wholewheat flour
4 large tomatoes – washed, roughly
  chopped
1 tablespoon tomato purée
¾ pt *(425 ml)* vegetable stock
1 dessertspoon mango chutney
lemon juice
salt and freshly ground pepper
8 eggs

1 Make the sauce: Soften the onion in a little oil in a saucepan until the onion is transparent, add the apple, curry powder and flour, stir well and cook for a few minutes.

2 Add all the other ingredients, gently simmer for 30–40 minutes until cooked and thicker.

3 Hard boil the eggs; put the eggs into cold water, bring to the boil reduce the heat then simmer for 12–15 minutes, drain and run under the cold tap until the eggs are cold, leave to stand in cold water until needed.

Serve by peeling the eggs and putting them whole in the curry sauce, then gently heat them through for a few minutes. Eaten with rice and other curry accompaniments it is an inexpensive and quick meal.

Stilton, Apple and Walnut Pasties

Pastry:
12 oz *(350 g)* wholewheat flour
6 oz *(175 g)* butter or margarine
a pinch of salt
4–5 tablespoons water

Filling:
8 oz *(225 g)* Stilton cheese
4 oz *(125 g)* cottage cheese
2 small cooking apples – washed, cored, roughly chopped
2 oz *(50 g)* walnuts – roughly chopped
2 tablespoons wholewheat breadcrumbs
salt and freshly ground pepper
1 egg – beaten

Oven: 425°f, 220°c, G.M.7

1 Make the pastry: Rub the fat into the flour and salt until it resembles fine breadcrumbs. Add enough water to bring the ingredients together into a soft ball.

2 Make the filling: Crumble the stilton into a bowl and mix in the other ingredients. Season well with salt and pepper to taste.

3 On a lightly floured surface with a floured rolling pin, roll out the pastry until it is about ¼" (6 mm) thick. Using a tea plate as a guide, cut out 4 circles.

4 Divide the mixture between the circles. Moisten the edges with a little of the beaten egg. Bring the edges up, seal well and crimp between your finger tips.

5 Stand the pasties on a greased baking tray, brush the pastry with the beaten egg.

Bake for 20–25 minutes until golden brown.

Cheese and Mushroom Pasties

Pastry:
12 oz *(350 g)* wholewheat flour
6 oz *(175 g)* butter or margarine
a pinch of salt
4–5 tablespoons water

Filling:
12 oz *(350 g)* curd cheese
4 oz *(125 g)* cottage cheese – drained
4 oz *(125 g)* button mushrooms –
    wiped, sliced
2 carrots – washed, finely grated
3 teaspoons horseradish sauce
salt and freshly ground pepper
fresh parsley – chopped

Decoration:
1 egg – beaten
sesame or poppy seeds

Oven: 425°f, 220°c, G.M.7

1 Make the pastry: Rub the fat into the flour and salt until it resembles fine breadcrumbs. Add enough water to make a soft dough.

2 Make the filling: Combine all the ingredients together in a bowl, season well with salt and pepper.

3 Roll the pastry out on a lightly floured surface using a floured rolling pin until it is about ¼″ (6 mm) thick. Using a tea plate as a guide cut out 4 circles.

4 Divide the filling mixture between the circles. Moisten the edges with a little of the beaten egg. Fold the pastry circles in half and seal the edges firmly together.

5 Grease a baking sheet, lay the pasties down, brush the tops with a little of the egg, sprinkle with sesame or poppy seeds.

Bake for 20–30 minutes until nicely browned.

These are ideal for picnics, packed lunches and light meals.

Cheesy Potato Cakes

1 lb *(450 g)* **fresh spinach, washed**
½ lb *(225 g)* **potatoes – washed**
½ lb *(225 g)* **hard cheese eg. cheddar – grated**
2 **egg yolks**
2 **teaspoons sage**
sea salt and freshly ground pepper

Coating:
2 **eggs – beaten**
2 oz *(50 g)* **medium oatmeal**
oil

1 Put whole washed potatoes into a saucepan of cold water with some salt. Cover and bring to the boil, reduce the heat and simmer for about 20 minutes until cooked. Test with a knife to see if they are cooked; the potatoes should slip easily off the blade when done.

2 De-stem the spinach: Fold the spinach along the spine of the leaf with the ridge on the outside. Pull the stem off right the way along the whole leaf.

3 Place the drained spinach in a covered saucepan with no extra water. Cook for 5–7 minutes over a moderate heat (younger leaves will cook quicker). Once cooked, drain well. Squeeze the spinach against the side of the saucepan with a wooden spoon to remove as much water as possible.

4 When the spinach is dry, roughly chop and season with salt and pepper and put to one side.

5 When cooked, mash the potatoes. Do not be tempted to use an electric liquidiser or processor for this as it makes the potato gluey. You might find bits of potato skin get caught in the masher; remove or stir back in as you wish. If the potatoes are peeled beforehand much of their vitamin content will be dissolved and lost in the cooking water.

6 Add the spinach to the potato, add the grated cheese followed by the yolks and sage. Taste and adjust the seasoning if required. Put the mixture in the fridge for a while, it will be easier to handle when cold.

7 Once cold, form the mixture into 8 rounds of even thickness and shape; this way they will cook evenly.

8 Coat the cakes: Beat the eggs in a bowl and put the oatmeal on a flat dish. One by one dip all the cakes in the egg making sure they are well covered, put on a plate. With clean hands, coat them in oatmeal, patting the oatmeal to make sure it sticks securely.

9 Heat enough oil to cover the bottom of a frying pan, fry the cakes in a moderate heat until nicely brown on both sides. Do not put too many in at once as it will make turn over difficult and will also reduce the heat of the oil.

Keep warm while the others cook, serve with homemade tomato sauce.

Florentine Eggs

1 lb *(450 g)* fresh spinach – washed

White sauce:
1 oz *(25 g)* butter or margarine
1 oz *(25 g)* potato flour (similar appearance and texture to cornflour) or wholewheat or cornflour
1 pt *(575 ml)* milk

Tomato sauce:
1 small onion – peeled, roughly chopped
oil
1 clove garlic – peeled, crushed
7 oz *(200 g)* tinned tomatoes
2 tablespoons tomato purée
1 bay leaf
½ teaspoon oregano
½ teaspoon basil
½ teaspoon thyme
salt and freshly ground pepper
6 eggs

Topping:
1 medium slice wholewheat bread –
crumbs
1 oz *(25 g)* **tasty cheese – grated**

Oven: 300°f, 150°c, G.M.2

1 Make the tomato sauce: Soften the onion and garlic in a little oil. When the onion is transparent add the other ingredients and simmer for 5–7 minutes until it becomes thick, stir occasionally so it does not stick to the bottom of the pan. Leave to cool.

2 Cook the eggs: Put them in a saucepan of cold water, bring them to the boil and simmer for ten minutes. After this, drain and run under the cold tap until the eggs are cold. Leave them to stand in cold water. This cooling helps prevent the grey ring from appearing between the yolk and the white.

3 Prepare the spinach: Fold along the spine of the leaf with the ridge on the outside. Pull the stem off right along the length of the leaf. Shake off any excess water. Put the leaves into a covered saucepan, no extra water is required. Cook for 5–7 minutes over a moderate heat until tender.

4 Drain well. Squeeze the spinach against the side of the pan with a wooden spoon to remove as much water as possible, this stops the finished dish from being soggy. Season the leaves with salt and pepper and place on the bottom of an ovenproof dish.

5 Remove the bay leaf from the tomato sauce, cover the spinach making an even layer.

6 Make the white sauce: Melt the fat in a saucepan, stir in the flour, cook this roux for a minute, remove from the heat and gradually add the milk, stir well to form a smooth sauce. Return to the heat, stirring all the time bring the sauce to the boil to thicken. Remove from the heat and season with salt and pepper.

7 Crack the eggs: Peel the eggs and slice in half lengthways, lay with the cut side down on the tomato sauce.

8 Spoon the sauce over the eggs.

9 Mix the breadcrumbs with the grated cheese and sprinkle over the top of the florentine.

Cook for 20–25 minutes to allow the ingredients to heat through.

Stilton, Apple, Celery and Walnut Soufflé

½ oz *(15 g)* butter or margarine
3 sticks celery – washed, thinly sliced
1 small cooking apple – washed,
    quartered, cored, diced
2 oz *(50 g)* walnuts – roughly chopped
½ oz *(15 g)* wholewheat flour
¼ pt *(150 ml)* milk
3 eggs
2 oz *(50 g)* Stilton – crumbled
salt and freshly ground pepper
1 tablespoon wholewheat
    breadcrumbs (optional)

Oven: 350°f, 150°c, G.M.4

1 Melt the butter or margarine in a saucepan and soften the celery. Once cooked, add the apple and the walnuts, turning them in the fat.

2 Add the flour and cook for a minute. Remove from the heat and stir in the milk, mixing thoroughly.

3 Return to the heat, and bring to the boil. Stir all the time. Remove from the heat once the sauce has thickened, allow to cool slightly, then stir in the Stilton. Season well.

4 Butter a 6″ (15 cm) soufflé dish.

5 Separate the egg yolks from the egg whites: mix the yolks into the cheese sauce and put the whites into a large bowl ready for whisking.

6 Whisk the whites until stiff but not dry; they need to be the same consistency as the sauce otherwise they will not combine very evenly.

7 Gently fold the whites into the sauce using a figure of eight movement so as not to knock out much air from the whites.

8 Hold the soufflé mix close to the soufflé dish; carefully pour in the mixture, and sprinkle the breadcrumbs over the top. If you pour the mixture in from a great height it has the same effect as heavy handling, that is the air is knocked out.

Bake for 20–25 minutes or until it has risen well and has browned nicely on the top. To check if it is cooked, give the dish a slight shake, if it wobbles alarmingly, give the soufflé a few minutes more.

Tzatsiki

½ pt (275 ml) plain yoghurt
½ cucumber – peeled, cut into small cubes
1 clove garlic – peeled, crushed
salt and pepper to taste
paprika to decorate

Combine all the ingredients together in a bowl, chill. Decorate with paprika just before serving, delicious served with Tabouli.

Yoghurt Pot Cake

1 x 5 fl oz (150 ml) pot of natural yoghurt
2 yoghurt pots of golden granulated sugar
2 yoghurt pots of wholewheat self-raising flour
1 yoghurt pot of ground almonds
1 yoghurt pot of sunflower oil
3 eggs
a few drops of natural almond essence
3 tablespoons of Apricot jam

Oven: 350°f, 180°c, G.M.4

Here you use the yoghurt pot for measuring the ingredients.

Grease two 8" (20 cm) sandwich cake tins.
1 Put all the ingredients together in a bowl and beat.
2 Divide the mixture between the 2 tins, bake for 30 minutes until golden brown and firm to the touch.
3 Cool out of the tin on a cooling rack. Once cold, sandwich together with the jam.

Golden Meringues

The quantities are easy to work out.
2 oz *(50 g)* golden granulated sugar
for each egg white
4 egg whites
8 oz *(225 g)* golden granulated sugar

Oven: 250°f, 130°c, G.M.1

Lay sheets of non-stick paper over the baking tins.

1 In a clean dry bowl, whisk the egg whites until stiff, they should stand in peaks when the beaters are lifted out of the bowl.

2 Add half the sugar gradually as you whisk, continue to whisk until the meringue becomes very stiff and shiny.

3 Add the rest of the sugar and whisk well again.

4 Using a teaspoon for small meringues or a dessertspoon for larger ones, spoon blobs of meringue onto the paper, easing the mixture off the spoon with your little finger.

Bake in the oven until the meringues are dry right the way through, give them a tap, they should sound hollow.

The time will depend on their size, small ones will take about 2–2½ hours.

Once cooked, leave to cool (you could always turn the oven off and leave the meringues in just to make sure they have dried out completely). Eat sandwiched together with whipped cream, or with a mousse, ice-cream, yoghurt or fruit fool.

Store in a dry air-tight container, somewhere dry.

Baked Custard with Apricots and Honey

3 eggs
¾ pt *(425 ml)* milk
2 oz *(50 g)* golden granulated sugar
1 vanilla pod (or vanilla essence)
8 oz *(225 g)* dried apricots soaked
runny honey to taste

Oven: 325°f, 170°c, G.M.3

1 Mix the eggs together lightly, add the vanilla essence if used. Do not get the mixture frothy as this will make an unattractive final texture.

2 Heat the milk, sugar and vanilla pod, stir all the time, bring up to the boil, then remove from the heat and cool slightly. Remove pod.

3 Pour the milk onto the eggs and mix gently to avoid bubbles. The eggs will begin to cook in the heat of the milk so the custard has to be strained to remove these bits.

4 Strain into the ovenproof dish, set this in a roasting tin which contains ½" (1½ cm) of hot water. This serves as protection for the delicate custard ensuring it cooks very gently in a steamy atmosphere. This set up is known as a Bain-marie.

Bake for 40 minutes. Check if it is cooked by giving the dish a gentle shake: the middle of the custard should no longer be liquid, though it will wobble still and there should be a golden brown skin on the top.

1 Soak the apricots for at least 1 hour but preferably overnight for a thick sauce full of flavour.

2 Put the apricots and the soaking water into a saucepan, simmer gently for 10–15 minutes until tender.

3 Flavour with honey, serve warm with the custard.

Cheese Bread Rolls

½ oz *(15 g)* fresh yeast *(¼ oz (7 g)* dried yeast)
1 teaspoon sugar
8 oz *(225 g)* strong wholewheat flour
1 teaspoon of salt
a pinch of cumin
pepper
2 oz *(50 g)* margarine
3½ fl oz *(90 ml)* milk
2 eggs – beaten

Oven: 425°f, 200°c, G.M.7   4 oz *(125 g)* Sage Derby – grated

1 Rub the margarine into the flour with the salt, cumin and pepper and leave somewhere warm.

2 Warm the milk to blood temperature. Test with a finger.

3 Mix the yeast and sugar together, add the milk and put to one side to ferment. If using dried yeast, dissolve the sugar in half the warm milk, sprinkle the yeast over the top and leave in a warm place to ferment.

4 When the yeast is frothy and active add the beaten eggs to the yeast, add this mixture to the warm flour and mix well.

5 Turn out onto a floured surface and knead until smooth, return to the bowl, cover with a damp cloth or put the bowl inside a plastic bag, leave somewhere warm to rise for an hour. You will find it does not rise like normal bread.

1 Sprinkle the cheese over the risen dough then knock back by kneading.

2 Divide the dough into 6 equal pieces and shape into rolls.

3 Place on a greased baking tray in a close circle with one in the middle. Put in a warm place to prove for 10–15 minutes covered with a dry cloth or put inside a plastic bag.

Bake for 30–35 minutes until they sound hollow when tapped underneath.

You can leave some of the cheese out of the dough and keep it for decoration: 5 minutes before the end of cooking, brush the rolls with a little milk, sprinkle the cheese over the top then return to the oven.

Natural Yoghurt

1 pt *(575 ml)* **warm water**
6 **heaped tablespoons dried milk powder**
5 fl oz *(150 ml)* **pot live yoghurt**

Using a yoghurt maker: These yoghurt makers are inexpensive and worth buying if you intend to make regular quantities.

1 Thoroughly mix the milk powder with the warm water, it is important to make sure the milk has completely dissolved before going onto the next stage otherwise the finished yoghurt will not have a smooth texture.

2 Mix a little of the milk with the live yoghurt to form a smooth paste. Gradually add the rest of the milk, mixing all the time.

3 Pour into the container(s) of the yoghurt maker, cover, and leave until it sets. The time will depend on the size, those with individual pots will take about 3 hours for example. I have a 1½ pt pot so I leave it overnight which makes a lovely thick yoghurt.

Using a Thermos flask:

1 Warm the inside of a large flask with boiling water, leave to stand.

2 Mix the milk powder with hot water, leave to cool to blood temperature. The temperature can be reduced quickly by stirring. Test the temperature with your finger, there should be no sensation of temperature – hot or cold.

3 Blend the live yoghurt with a little of the milk, when you have a smooth paste, gradually stir in the rest of the milk.

4 Tip the water out of the flask. Pour in the yoghurt mixture, screw on the top lightly and leave in a warm place (an airing cupboard for example) for at least 8 hours.

5 Once set, transfer to another container with a good lid and store in the fridge.

If you have the individual pot type maker you could make flavoured yoghurts by putting a teaspoon of natural jam in the bottom of the container before pouring on the milk and yoghurt mixture. It makes a change!

Nuts and Seeds

I love nuts and seeds, especially with sultanas. The combination of the sweetness of the fruit with the smooth texture and distinctive flavours of the nuts is delicious. Nuts contain a high percentage of fat, the worst culprits being brazils, cashews and peanuts, but, do not let that put you off. At least the fat is of the polyunsaturated type. Nuts are also high in concentrated protein, particularly pine nuts, almonds, pistachio nuts and sunflower seeds. As a group, nuts and seeds are richer in protein than the pulses; the disadvantage is that they are not consumed in large enough quantities, as in many cases, large amounts can be very indigestible, and of course they are very calorific. The answer therefore is to make the best use of what they provide by combining them with cheaper, less fattening ingredients like pulses, grains and vegetables thus making complete proteins.

It is important to include nuts in the diet because they include valuable mineral sources:

1. PHOSPHORUS which works with the B vitamins.
2. POTASSIUM which helps to regulate the blood pressure.
3. IRON needed to oxygenate the blood.
4. CALCIUM this is normally associated with dairy products but surprisingly, hazelnuts have particularly high levels. Weight for weight, they contain more than dried milk. Sesame seeds are an alternative source.

Supplies of vitamins found in nuts and seeds
1. B vitamins are found in almonds, brazils, pine nuts, peanuts and pistachio nuts.
2. Vitamin E – Chestnuts contain this and are the only nut to contain significant carbohydrates, which are present in an important unprocessed form. Chestnuts are very versatile and can be made into pâté, combined with other ingredients to make casseroles and pies or puréed to make puddings, for example, mixed together with butter, orange and sugar they make a simple, quick but luxurious mousse. Sunflower seeds contain this vitamin too.
3. Vitamin C. It is strange to think of nuts containing a vitamin

usually associated with citrus fruits, but this vitamin is present in cashew nuts.

4 Vitamin D, found in sunflower seeds is needed for the absorption of calcium and phosphorus required for healthy bones and teeth.

BUYING AND STORAGE

With the growing interest in wholefoods, the necessity for more varieties of nuts has meant shops now stock types from all corners of the world.

1. Nuts and seeds are only sold when they are ripe and therefore fully mature, this means they will be at the height of their nutritional value. It must be said that the only way from this point is down. Even though deterioration is a relatively slow process, always buy from a shop with a good turnover of stock, and do not be tempted to buy in too big a quantity; little and often is the best policy in this case.

2. It is true to say that nuts will be fresher and keep better if they are bought in their shells, but unfortunately, I am sure very few people have the time to stand cracking nuts every time a few ounces are needed for a recipe. More's the pity! Therefore for the sake of convenience, buy the shelled nuts for cooking and keep others for when you have time to enjoy them properly.

3. Look out for brightly coloured nuts, avoid the ones that appear dull, tired and oily looking; these will almost certainly be on the stale side and could well taste bitter.

4. Always buy nuts in their brown skins; without this protective layer they quickly start to lose their natural oils. If you do have to remove this layer, as with almonds for decoration purposes, just pour boiling water over the amount needed, wait a few minutes, then gently squeeze the nut between your index finger and thumb, the skin is easily shed this way. If the skin is left on it will not impair the flavour, in fact I think it heightens the nutty taste and of course it does mean the nut will retain its quality and goodness. Having said all that, there are recipes that do require the skins to be removed, and peanut butter is one of these. Peanuts are skinned very simply by roasting the

nuts on a flat tray in a hot oven for about 20 minutes. The skins
are easily made to flake off the nuts by rubbing hands full of
nuts in a dry tea towel. Do not be tempted to use your bare
hands, it is surprising how much heat the nuts can hold.

5. It is obviously much cheaper to buy broken nuts like walnuts,
cashews and brazils. Nine times out of ten the recipe will state
chopped nuts, so this way you are half way there.

6. Chesnuts might well not be the first example that springs to
mind when nuts are mentioned, they are however extremely
versatile and come in a variety of forms.

   a) Fresh nuts are available during the winter months. They are
   unfortunately quite a performance to prepare, so, unless you
   intend roasting them in the fire, why not try a tinned variety
   first, acquire the taste, then launch out on the fresh.

   b) Chestnut purée – is available in most good, big supermarkets. It comes in sweetened and unsweetened forms, so do
   check the label. Do not despair if you can only find the
   sweetened type and you want to use it for something
   savoury. I have used it in pâté and it did not seem to have a
   dreadful effect on the final dish, although the plain variety
   would be preferable of course.

   c) Whole canned chestnuts are sold in plain water and would be
   a tasty addition to casseroles, stews and pies, or you can
   make your own purée by putting them through the
   liquidiser or food processor.

   d) Dried chestnuts are available in some shops. They will need
   soaking for at least three hours, by which time they will
   double in size and weight. They have a rich sweet taste, far
   more so than the canned product. Their rich flavour makes a
   delicious addition to a thick winter stew.

7. Coconut is something you might not have considered using
very much in cooking until now. True coconut is not that sweet
sticky processed stuff, which bears no resemblance to the fresh.
Freshly grated coconut flesh has the most wonderful taste,
luscious, moist and chewy; it is an experience that should not
only be restricted to winnings from a coconut shy. Proobably a
more practical alternative would be the dried flakes of coconut
flesh on sale in all health food shops. These will add an
interesting crunch to salads and by toasting them under the
grill they will make a lovely addition to muesli. There is also a
product available called coconut cream which comes in the

form of a hard vaccum packed block or in a can. It is a traditional addition or accompaniment for curries and Indian style pulse dishes, and like finely grated or dessicated coconut, it can be added to cakes, biscuits or puddings. It is possible to make a sort of cream by whisking 3 ounces (75 g) of the coconut cream with ¼ pint (150 ml) of warm water until it thickens. This is an alternative topping for puddings and is especially useful for Vegans who prefer not to eat any animal products.

8. Once you have bought your supply of nuts, keep them cool and dry in air-tight containers. They have to be sealed containers as nuts tend to absorb flavours and smells from the atmosphere around them.

9. You will often see chopped nuts in supermarkets; these are not a good idea to buy. As with anything that is prepared a long time in advance, much of the goodness soon disappears. Therefore chop nuts as you require them.

The best way to chop nuts is to use a heavy chopping knife as this way there will be very little chance of overgrinding the nuts. It is quicker (especially as the quantities of nuts involved are usually only a few ounces) and you will not have a fiddly liquidiser goblet to clean, with nut purée caked around the blades. Moreover hand chopped nuts give the final dish a far nicer texture and appearance. Obviously, if you have large quantities to chop as for peanut butter, a food processor or liquidiser is acceptable. The oil that you add helps the nuts whizz more quickly and smoothly without clogging the blades, reducing the chance of overgrinding the nuts which has a tendency to make them go oily and could ruin the final product.

NUT AND SEED PREPARATIONS

1. Butters

Peanut butter as made by wholefood manufacturers is THE most delicious spread, dare I say, eaten by the spoonful on its own (!) in sandwiches, on toast or used in biscuits, savoury patties and in salad dressings. Making seeds and nuts into butters like this is an excellent way of providing a nutritious sandwich filling and is a way of making them more easily digested as the grinding helps to break down the fats which make up a large proportion of the nutritional content. Watch out for some popular brands of peanut butter as they contain salt, sugar and stabilisers. They are a light brown colour with very little in the way of texture, and their taste is no match for the nutty brown, crunchy wholefood brands. The method of making nut and seed butter is simple so you can experiment with different combinations of nuts and seeds. All are gently roasted, then ground with a good quality oil and seasoned with a little sea salt if required. Then store your butter in an airtight jar.

2. *Nut and Seed Oils*
Just like other oils, they can be used for cooking and salad dressings. SAFFLOWER is the highest in polyunsaturated fats in this group, this is closely followed by SUNFLOWER which has the added bonus of being cheaper. GROUND NUT (peanut or Arachide) oil is becoming far more readily available, even in supermarkets, it is not quite as good as sunflower, but it does have a very distinctive flavour usually associated with chinese food.

SESAME SEED oil is very expensive but it is worth it for it has a deep amber colour, it has a slightly bitter taste like Tahini the sesame seed spread made from puréed seeds in the same way as peanut butter. A special occasion type of oil would be WALNUT or HAZELNUT. Both have a rich, full flavour and are best kept for salad dressings so their fine flavour can be fully appreciated.

3. *Sprouting Seeds*
The same method applies as for sprouting pulses, see chart.

TABLE OF NUTS AND SEEDS – 1

TYPE	ORIGIN	SHELL	KERNEL	TASTE/TEXTURE	INFORMATION
ALMOND	Cultivated in the Mediterranean, N. Africa, S. Africa, Australia & California.	Oval, golden brown with pin-pricked appearance.	1" long, mid-brown in colour, flat & oval.	Sweet, pronounced taste.	2 types of Almonds, bitter & sweet; only sell sweet – other poisonous. Sold: whole, split, flaked & ground.
BRAZIL	Brazil, Venezuela, Chile, Africa. Fruit grows at top of tall trees, weighs 4 lbs, contains 20 nuts.	Greyish brown, 3 sided ridged texture. 1½–2" long.	Dappled ivory & brown.	Rich creamy taste, smooth firm texture.	Best season, Nov–Feb. Avoid those in shells which rattle.
CASHEW	Cultivated in India & E. Africa. Extraordinary growth – a large apple with kidney-shaped, olive coloured single nut hanging from it.	Sold without shell as surrounded by poisonous acid.	Whitish in colour, rounded kidney shape ¼"–1" long.	Bland, but a pleasant flavour, slightly sweet. A smooth texture.	Sold: whole, roasted, salted, halved (cheaper) pieces are good for cooking. Cheapest is ground, can be used in same way as ground almonds.
SWEET CHESTNUTS	Cultivated in Spain, Italy & France. Not to be confused with Horse Chesnuts or Conkers!	Prickly green covering that is removed.	Shiny brown & triangular in shape, skinned before eating.	Distinctive 'mealy' texture, with strong flavour.	Chestnut purée in tins or tubes, sweetened or unsweetened. Dried Chestnut – kernel looks small & yellow.

TABLE OF NUTS AND SEEDS – 2

TYPE	ORIGIN	SHELL	KERNEL	TASTE/TEXTURE	INFORMATION
COCONUTS	Grow best near sea, familiar sight in India, Malaysia, W. Africa. Found at top of tall palm trees.	Size of grapefruit – oval shape with hard brown shell covered with mat of fibrous threads.	Flesh is white. Contains liquid or milk.	Moist, creamy taste. Coarse texture.	Mature nuts do not have the clear 'milk'. *Desiccated*: fresh shredded flesh, dried. Use in baking. *Strands*: or chips or shreds – different forms of desiccated coconut. *Cream*: hard white fat. Added to curries.
HAZELNUTS (COB NUTS or FILBERTS)	Grown throughout Europe.	Fresh from tree, they are contained in greeny brown case, usually small, golden brown and shiny.	Size of large pea, pointed at one end. White on outside when younger, get darker with age.	Firm texture skin can sometimes be a little bitter.	Available all year, can be roasted or ground.
PEANUTS (GROUND NUTS, MONKEY NUTS)	Grown in most hot countries	Curvy beige-coloured tubes, which are easily broken	Small ovals covered in reddish brown skin. This skin easily removed by roasting.	Wonderful taste enhanced by roasting, dry roasting & salting.	Cheap form of protein, packed with vital nutrients.

TABLE OF NUTS AND SEEDS – 3

TYPE	ORIGIN	SHELL	KERNEL	TASTE/TEXTURE	INFORMATION
PECAN	Cultivated in Australia, Israel & S. Africa.	Smooth, shiny & reddish brown, easily cracked.	Looks rather like elongated Walnut.	Sweet flavour, fleshy texture.	Contain useful amounts of vitamin A, but are fairly calorific.
PINE KERNELS (PIGNOLIAS, INDIAN NUT)	Come from STONE PINE tree grown on Mediterranean coastline.	Sold without shell.	½" long, creamy-white in colour. Cylindrical shape.	Unusual aromatic flavour, soft oily texture.	Generally expensive. Important ingredient in PESTO with garlic oil & basil – a sauce served with pasta in Italy.
PISTACHIO	Central Asia, Persia.	A reddish brown outer case.	Bright green, really attractive looking nut.	Pleasant but bland taste.	The greener the kernel, the better the quality. Colour & flavour plus excellent keeping qualities make them expensive.
WALNUTS	S.W. Europe, Central Asia.	Round in shape, beige in colour coming in two pieces	Comes in two intricately shaped sections joined in the centre.	Dark, rich unmistakable flavour.	Available all year round. They are very nutritious & are rich in oil.

Peanut, Carrot and Tomato Soup

4 oz *(125 g)* shelled peanuts
1 onion – peeled, roughly chopped
1 lb carrots – washed, roughly sliced
1 lb tomatoes – washed, roughly
   chopped
1 clove garlic – peeled, crushed
1 tablespoon oil
1½ pts *(850 ml)* vegetable stock
1 teaspoon basil (dried)
salt and pepper
freshly chopped parsley for
   decoration

1 Soften the onion, garlic and carrot in a little oil in a covered saucepan. Cook until the onion is soft and transparent.

2 Add the peanuts, tomatoes and basil, simmer over a low heat for 10 minutes.

3 Pour on the stock and simmer for a further 10 minutes. Season with salt and pepper and serve decorated with the parsley.

If you want a smooth texture to the soup, put it through a liquidiser, return to the heat before serving to warm through.

Peanut Butter

8 oz *(225 g)* peanuts – unroasted,
   shelled
2 tablespoons good oil – sunflower or
   peanut (arachide)
a pinch of salt

Oven: 350°f, 180°c, G.M.4

1 Spread the nuts evenly out on a baking tray.

2 Cook for 20 minutes, turn occasionally. Remove the tray and allow to cool for a few minutes.

3 In a dry clean tea towel rub the skins off small handfuls of the nuts, and put the skinned nuts into a liquidiser goblet or processor.

4 When all the nuts are skinned, grind down until quite fine. You will have to stop frequently to scrape the sides down.

5 Add the oil and work into a smooth paste.

Season with salt and store in a jam jar. This amount will almost fill a 1 lb jar.

The roasting is important. The nuts need to have a good colour otherwise the butter will not have much of a taste, but this does not mean they should be on the lighter side of burnt!

Mixed Nut and Seed Roast

2 large onions – peeled, roughly
    chopped
3 oz *(75 g)* sunflower seeds
1 oz *(25 g)* pumpkin seeds
6 oz *(175 g)* mixed nuts, brazils,
    almonds, walnuts, cashew,
    peanuts – finely chopped
oil
2 large carrots – washed, grated
4 oz *(125 g)* wholewheat breadcrumbs
½ pt *(275 ml)* vegetable stock (or
    Vecon/yeast extract)
½ teaspoon mace
½ teaspoon cumin
1 teaspoon ginger
salt and freshly ground pepper

Oven: 350°f, 180°c, G.M.4

1 Heat a small amount of oil in a frying pan. Add the onions and chopped nuts and seeds, and gently fry until the onions are transparent.

2 Grate the carrots into a bowl, add the breadcrumbs and spices, add the onion and nuts and seeds once cooked, pour over the vegetable stock and mix well. Season with salt and freshly ground pepper.

3 Put the mixture into a greased soufflé dish or pie dish, press down firmly.

Bake for 35–45 minutes until firm and brown on the top.

Eat hot or cold, ideal with salad or for picnics.

Nut Stuffed Cabbage Leaves with Tomato Sauce

8 large cabbage leaves (Savoy type i.e. not white cabbage) – unblemished, washed
8 oz *(225 g)* brown rice – washed
1 onion – peeled, roughly chopped
1 clove garlic – peeled, crushed
1 large tomato – washed, roughly chopped
1 oz *(25 g)* pine nuts
1 oz *(25 g)* walnuts – chopped
1 oz *(25 g)* almonds – chopped
1 oz *(25 g)* currants
1 teaspoon thyme
salt and freshly ground pepper
2 tablespoons parsley – chopped
2 teaspoons mint sauce concentrate
oil
vegetable stock

Tomato sauce:
1½ lbs *(700 g)* ripe tomatoes (or tinned tomatoes)
1 onion – peeled, roughly chopped
1 clove garlic – peeled, crushed
½ teaspoon basil
½ teaspoon thyme
½ teaspoon marjoram

Oven: 350°f, 180°c, G.M.4

1 Make the sauce: Soften the onion and garlic in a little oil in a saucepan, cook until the onion is transparent. Add all the other sauce ingredients and simmer for 30 minutes. Once cooked, liquidise to make a smooth sauce. Season with salt and pepper and leave to one side.

2 Make the stuffing: In a saucepan, heat a small amount of oil, soften the onion and garlic, when transparent, add the rice and turn into the oil, cook for 3 minutes.

3 Add the chopped tomato, nuts, currants and herbs. Cook for a minute.

4 Add enough water to come 1½ inches above the level of the rice. Bring the saucepan upto the boil, reduce the heat and simmer for about 30 minutes until the stock has been absorbed. (Bring the saucepan to the boil with the lid on, put the lid half on during the 30 minutes, then remove the lid completely towards the end of the cooking to evaporate any remaining liquid).

5 Once the rice is cooked, season well with salt and pepper, add the mint, cover and leave to one side while the cabbage leaves are prepared.

6 Blanch the cabbage: Bring a saucepan of water upto the boil. Cook the leaves for 1–2 minutes to make them softer. Drain and run them under the cold tap to stop any further cooking. Then drain again (this is known as 'refreshing').

7 With a sharp knife, shave away a little of the outside of the thick part of the stem from each leaf, this will make them easier to fold.

8 Turn each leaf over so that the inside of the leaf is uppermost. Divide the mixture between the leaves.

9 Folding the leaves: With the stem nearest you, fold over the bottom of the leaf. Fold over the sides almost to the middle, this will enclose the stuffing. Roll the leaf up from the stem to the top making a neat parcel.

10 Place these parcels in an ovenproof dish, with the flap underneath to stop them unrolling.

11 Pour over the tomato sauce, add enough vegetable stock to bring the braising (cooking) liquid just to the top of the parcels.

12 Cover and cook for an hour. Serve with the tomato sauce that the leaves were cooked in.

Savoury Nut Cakes

4 oz *(125 g)* **Sunflower seeds**
4 oz *(125 g)* **mixed nuts eg. brazils, peanuts, cashew, almonds, walnuts**
4 tablespoons oatmeal
6–8 tablespoons boiling water
¼ teaspoon Vecon or yeast extract
1 teaspoon mixed herbs
1 teaspoon ground mace
salt and pepper
2 eggs

Coating:
Beaten egg
seasoned wholewheat flour

1 Finely chop the nuts and seeds (carefully grind in a liquidiser or food processor if you prefer a very smooth texture).

2 Put the nuts, seeds and oatmeal in a bowl, season with the herbs, mace, salt and freshly ground pepper.

3 Add the vegcon to the boiling water, mix well then add to the oatmeal and nut mix. Add enough egg to make a soft but manageable dough. Chill for 30 minutes or so.

4 Divide the dough into 8 equal sized pieces mould into cakes of an even shape and depth (this will mean they will cook evenly).

5 Beat the eggs for the coating (remember to add any egg that might be left over from the mixture). Season some wholewheat flour with salt and pepper, put on a flat dish.

6 Dip all the cakes in the egg. Wash and dry your hands to prevent a sticky mess. Coat the cakes in the flour, pat to make sure the coating has stuck and that any excess comes off, this will only burn in the oil otherwise.

7 Heat enough oil to just cover the bottom of a frying pan. When it is hot (you can test this by putting a few crumbs of oatmeal into the fat, if they sizzle, the fat is hot enough).

Put the cakes in and cook for a couple of minutes until golden brown. Do not overcrowd the pan as this will make turning the cakes more difficult and the cooking will be slower. Cook a few at a time, then once brown, remove and keep warm while cooking the rest.

Serve with homemade tomato sauce or ratatouille for example.

For a more pronounced 'nutty' flavour, gently toast the nuts and seeds before you chop them.

Quick Nut Loaf

1 onion – peeled, roughly chopped
4 oz *(125 g)* brazil nuts – roughly chopped
4 oz *(125 g)* peanuts – roughly chopped
oil
5 oz *(150 g)* wholewheat breadcrumbs
6 large tomatoes – washed, roughly chopped (or a 15 oz *(425 g)* tin of tomatoes)
3 tablespoons oatmeal
3 tablespoons jumbo oats
½ pt *(275 ml)* tomato juice
1 teaspoon mixed herbs
½ teaspoon basil
½ teaspoon thyme
salt and freshly ground pepper
Worcester sauce

Oven: 350°f, 180°c, G.M.4

Grease a 1½ lb loaf tin or an ovenproof dish.

1 Heat a small amount of oil in a frying pan, add the onions and the chopped nuts. Fry over a moderate heat until the onion is transparent.

2 Collect the other ingredients together in a bowl. When the onions are cooked, add to the bowl and mix very well. Season to taste with the salt, pepper and Worcester sauce.

3 Transfer to the cooking container and press firmly into the dish.

Bake for 40–50 minutes until firm and brown on the top.

Can be served hot or cold

Mixed Nut and Vegetable Risotto

1 large onion – peeled, roughly
   chopped
4 medium carrots – washed, sliced
4 large sticks celery – washed, sliced
1 red pepper – washed, deseeded,
   roughly cubed
1 green pepper – washed, deseeded,
   roughly cubed
6 oz *(175 g)* mixed nuts – walnuts,
   brazils, cashew, almonds –
   roughly chop large nuts
oil
10 oz *(275 g)* brown rice
3 teaspoons paprika
1½ pts *(850 ml)* vegetable stock
6 oz *(175 g)* sweetcorn kernels
2 tablespoons chopped parsley
salt and freshly ground pepper

1 In a large uncovered saucepan soften the vegetables with the nuts in a little oil, over a low heat until the onion is transparent.

2 Once cooked add the rice and the paprika, cook for a further 2 minutes stirring regularly to prevent the paprika from sticking.

3 Add the stock, cover, and bring to the boil, add the sweetcorn, reduce to a simmer.

4 Keep on the lowest heat and cook for 45 minutes until the stock has been absorbed.

5 Turn off the heat, leave the saucepan covered and untouched for a further 10 minutes.

6 Season with salt and freshly ground pepper, stir in the parsley.

Any vegetables can be used in this dish – swede, turnip, parsnip, whatever you have to hand. Two things to remember, keep it colourful and if using anything like courgettes, tomatoes, mushrooms etc, keep these until the stock has been brought to the boil, otherwise they will be cooked to destruction.

Nutty Fruit Crumble

1½ lbs *(700 g)* **seasonal fruit**
2 tablespoons honey

Crumble:
5 oz *(150 g)* **wholewheat flour**
2 oz *(50 g)* **butter or margarine**
2 tablespoons Barbados sugar
½ teaspoon mixed spice
2 oz *(50 g)* **walnuts – roughly chopped**

Oven: 400°f, 200°c, G.M.6

1 Prepare the desired fruit accordingly. Slice or arrange in the bottom of an ovenproof dish, spoon over the honey.
2 Rub the fat into the flour until it resembles fine breadcrumbs.
3 Stir in the sugar, mixed spice and walnuts.
4 Cover the fruit with the crumble.

Bake for 35–40 minutes until the top is nicely brown.

Serve warm with cream, yoghurt or custard.

Coconut Bars

2 oz *(50 g)* **butter**
2 oz *(50 g)* **margarine**
3 oz *(75 g)* **wholewheat flour**
4 oz *(100 g)* **desiccated coconut**
1 oz *(25 g)* **Barbados sugar**
1 teaspoon baking powder

Oven: 375°f, 190°c, G.M.5

Makes 8 bars

1 Melt the fat in a saucepan.
2 Once melted, add all the other ingredients and stir very well until everything is coated in the fat.
3 Grease a square baking tin approximately 7" (18 cm) square.

4 Press the mixture into the tin, smooth the top with a knife.

Bake for 20–25 minutes until golden brown.

Carefully mark into 8 fingers. The mixture is very fragile so leave to cool completely in the tin, then store in an air-tight container.

Luxury Nut and Coffee Cake

Topping:
4 oz *(125 g)* mixed nuts eg. cashew, walnuts, almonds, brazils – roughly chopped
3 oz *(75 g)* Demerara sugar
3 oz *(75 g)* butter or margarine
1 tablespoon water
1 teaspoon instant coffee

Cake:
8 oz *(225 g)* wholewheat flour
2 teaspoons baking powder
3 oz *(75 g)* butter or margarine
3 oz *(75 g)* Demerara sugar
4 fl oz *(125 ml)* milk
1 medium egg
2 tablespoons water
2 teaspoons instant coffee

Oven: 350°f, 180°c, G.M.4

1 Grease well a 7–8"(18–20 cm) deep cake tin. Not one with a loose bottom or you will lose all the delicious topping. An alternative would be a 1½ lb loaf tin.

2 Put all the topping ingredients into a saucepan and melt gently. Once the fat has melted, pour into the prepared tin, spread evenly over the bottom.

3 Rub the fat into the flour and baking powder in a bowl. Add the sugar and mix well.

4 Combine the milk, egg, water and coffee together. Gradually add to the flour and stir well to form a soft mixture that will easily drop off the spoon. More water might be required.

5 Spoon the sponge onto the topping and smooth the surface.

Bake in the middle of the oven for 35–45 minutes.

Check after 30 minutes. Slip a knife into the middle of the cake, take care not to push it as far down as the sticky topping, if the blade comes out clean the cake is done.

When the cake is cooked, loosen the edge of the cake away from the tin with a knife. Turn out onto a cooling rack. If any nuts remain in the tin, scoop them out and place back on the top, they will soon set.

Sesame Oatcake

6 oz *(175 g)* **butter or margarine**
1 tablespoon black treacle
4 oz *(125 g)* **golden granulated sugar**
6 oz *(175 g)* **medium oatmeal**
10 oz *(275 g)* **jumbo oats**
a pinch of salt
1 tablespoon sesame seeds

Oven: 325°f, 170°c, G.M.3

1 Melt the fat and the treacle over a gentle heat in a large saucepan.

2 Once the fat has melted, stir in the sugar, when this is well combined, add all the other ingredients.

3 Grease a baking tin 10 x 14" (25½ x 35½ cms). Spread the mixture evenly in the tin, press down firmly so everything sticks together.

Bake for 20 minutes until a deep brown, be careful because it can burn easily.

Once out of the oven, immediately mark into 12 squares or 16 fingers. Leave to cool for five minutes to allow the treacle to set a little then take out of the tin and cool on a wire rack.

Chocolate and Walnut Brownies

4 oz *(125 g)* **butter or margarine**
1 oz *(25 g)* **carob powder**
6 tablespoons of water
4 oz *(125 g)* **golden granulated sugar**
2 oz *(50 g)* **walnuts – roughly chopped**
a pinch of salt
4 oz *(125 g)* **self raising wholewheat flour (add 1 teaspoon of baking powder if using plain flour)**
2 eggs

Oven: 325°f, 170°c, G.M.3

Makes 8 big or 16 smaller pieces.

Grease an 8" (20 cm) square baking tin.

1 Put the fat, carob, water, sugar, walnuts and salt into a saucepan over a low heat, stirring occasionally.

2 Once the fat has melted, remove from the heat, add the flour (and baking powder if used) and mix well.

3 Add the eggs mixing well. The mixture will thicken slightly. Pour into the baking tin.

Bake in the middle of the oven for 30–35 minutes. When cooked it will be firm to the touch, if unsure test with a knife, if it comes out clean the brownies are done.

Divide into 8 or 16 pieces, leave in the tin for a few minutes, then cool on a cooling rack.

Flavourings

OILS, VINEGARS, HERBS AND SPICES

Having gone to all the trouble of ensuring that your vegetables, fruit, pulses, grains, nuts and seeds are in first class condition, you will not want to spoil the final dish by using poor quality flavourings. They are a very important consideration in cooking and need looking after so that they give the best possible result at all times.

1. Oils

Oils are the fatty substances that remain liquid at room temperature. However, if stored in a cold cupboard, some types have a tendency to go slightly solid and cloudy, but they quickly revert back to their normal state once they have been returned to room temperature.

There are many different types of oil, some are refined to such a degree that very little flavour remains, and at the other extreme, some have a rich, distinctive taste. It is a question of personal preference.

a) OLIVE OIL

Good olive oil is fragrant with a full, rich flavour which is absorbed by the food. The very best quality is known as Virgin oil. This has come from the first pressing of fresh, green olives, which results in a dark green coloured oil with a wonderful aroma. It is however expensive, so is best kept for salad dressings, mayonnaise etc where its full flavour can be appreciated.

The second pressing extracts an oil that is a pale yellow colour. Its flavour is not as fine as the Virgin, so it can be used for sautéing (shallow frying), dressings and mayonnaise.

Low grade olive oil is made from crushed olives that have been heated and pressed. Flavourwise, it does not compare with the other two, but it has a variety of uses.

b) OLIVETTE

Sometimes called salad oil, it is made from a mixture of olive and corn oils. The flavour is not that good, but the addition of the corn oil does mean it can be taken to a higher temperature, which is a requirement for frying.

c) CORN OIL
This is extracted from sweetcorn kernels. It has no taste, so if used, keep only for frying. It too has a low decomposition property enabling high temperatures to be reached without burning.

d) GROUNDNUT (Peanut or Arachide) OIL
Originally, peanut oil had rather an over-powering taste, this has been tempered slightly through improved refining techniques, making it acceptable for salad dressings, sautéing etc.

e) SUNFLOWER OIL
Made from the seeds of the sunflower, this oil has a light, nutty flavour which makes a lovely alternative if you are not too keen on the richness of olive oil. It is suitable for all preparations. If you intend to deep fry – use a cheaper oil.

f) SESAME SEED OIL
Made from sesame seeds, and like all products from this source, it is full of flavour, rich and nutty tasting. It is commonly used in Middle Eastern and Chinese cooking.

g) WALNUT OR HAZELNUT OIL
These are the finest oils and are consequently expensive, but well worth it for special occasions as you can really taste the quality.

h) SAFFLOWER OIL
This is made from the flowers of false saffron. The oil is nutty and so is ideal for dressings as well as cooking.

Storage
They need to be kept in a cool dark place, otherwise the light tends to make them go rancid after a period of time. Don't worry, oils will keep for about six months without turning sour.

2. Vinegar
Vinegar is an acid liquid made from the sour fermentation of wine, cider or malt. Its main application is in dressings, such as vinaigrettes, or mayonnaise, where it gives a distinctive yet subtle, well rounded flavour, enhancing the dish concerned.

To add an individual taste to your vinegar, it is quite simple to make herb vinegars at home. First, steep fresh herbs in either wine or cider vinegar for 10 days or more, until a full flavour is achieved. The herbs are then strained off and the liquid bottled, often with a sprig of fresh herbs for decoration and easy identification. The best result will come from using the best possible ingredients.

Suitable herbs are: basil, borage, dill, fennel, lemon balm, marjoram, mint, tarragon, rosemary, chives for red and white vinegars. Tarragon, basil and mint for cider vinegar.

Method.
1. Chop or bruise the herb by rubbing them through your fingers.
2. Put into a jar, cover with vinegar and leave in a dark place.
3. Shake everyday for 10 days.
4. Strain into a good screw top jar or corked bottle.

Flavoured vinegars can be made in the same way using seeds like coriander and dill. Bruise 1–2 ounces of seed with a rolling pin, put into a jar, cover with 2 pints of warm vinegar, cover, store in a warm place for 2 weeks, shake from time to time, strain.

HERB OILS can be made in the same way as these vinegars, 2 tablespoons of herb to ½ pint of oil, stand in strong light for 2–3 weeks, and shake twice a day.

To test the herb oils and vinegars, drop some on the back of your hand, it should smell of the herb. If not, strain the liquid off the old herbs, and repeat the process with some more fresh herbs.

3. *Herbs*

Herbs are an essential element in cooking, be they dried or fresh, which is preferable. Without their distinctive flavour, dishes would be sadly lacking. Fresh herbs can be a great asset when presenting foods, as their fresh colour, interesting shapes and textures really help to lift the final result, making it look appetising and complete.

There are the classical combinations like basil and tomatoes, but, as with everything, it is all a matter of personal choice and makes a marvellous opportunity to experiment for different effects and tastes.

One point to remember, dried herbs are more potent than the fresh variety, so where you might add tablespoons of freshly chopped herbs, this will be translated in terms of teaspoons for dried herbs. Keep them in a cool, dark place.

Make sure they are and look as fresh as possible with a good colour, not wilting and dry as so often is the case. Keep them in a screw top jar in the bottom of the fridge for up to a week. To use – remove leaves from stalks and roughly chop.

TABLE OF HERBS – 1

HERB	APPEARANCE	FLAVOUR	USES
BAY LEAF	Fairly large deep green leaf. Paler when dried.	Pleasant aromatic flavour, makes good background flavour.	Should not be overdone, easy addition to stews, casseroles, soups, stock & infused with milk for savoury sauces.
BASIL	2 types: Bush & Sweet, latter considered best. It is a thin-stemmed plant with many green leaves which often have a purple tinge to them.	Fresh: Leaves have delicate distinctive flavour. Dried: Stronger more concentrated taste.	Goes particularly well with Mediterranean type dishes using tomatoes, aubergine & courgette.
CHIVES	Long & thin, they look more like blades of grass.	Has delicate onion flavour.	Can be used in abundance. Excellent with egg & cheese dishes, ideal for salads & snipped it makes a good decoration.
CORIANDER	Very pretty leaf not unlike parsley – slightly bigger.	Mild flavour.	Chopped – can be used in curry, Middle Eastern dishes, makes pretty decoration.
DILL	Has a feathery bluish-green leaf like fennel.	It has a sweet slightly pungent flavour not unlike Caraway.	DILL WEED: Can be used in tomato, bean & pea dishes, or as decoration. DILL SEEDS: Used in casseroles, stews etc.

TABLE OF HERBS – 2

HERB	APPEARANCE	FLAVOUR	USES
FENNEL	The long root produces a short grooved stem, this is ideal finely sliced in salads. The feathery leaves are very attractive. The dried seeds are small & fawn in colour.	Root: subtle, aniseed. Leaves: aniseed with a hint of smokiness. Seeds: Dry perfumed aniseed.	ROOT: salad, stir fried vegetables. LEAVES: salad, decoration. SEEDS: used in stocks.
GARLIC	The bulb consists of individual cloves enclosed by a white skin. A single clove is usually enough per recipe.	Strong, distinctive flavour, has definite after taste, and smell!!	Has health properties – stimulates digestive organs, aiding blood pressure & circulation. Use sparingly as general flavouring in dishes.
HORSERADISH	This root is cultivated in West Asia, it is long & white.	It has a definite taste with a hot flavour.	Peeled and grated it can be added to mayonnaise & lentil dishes.
MARJORAM	2 types: Pot & Sweet. The leaves are small with a grey down. There are red or white flowers from July to September.	Both have a sweet slightly spicy flavour.	Good with tomato, especially Italian type dishes.
MINT	Spearmint or Applemint. Pale green hairy leaves with crinkly appearance.	Refreshing light flavour.	Used in cooking water for potatoes & peas. Can be chopped & sprinkled over cooked vegetables, salads, added to sauces, vinaigrette & pulse dishes.

TABLE OF HERBS – 3

HERB	APPEARANCE	FLAVOUR	USES
OREGANO	Is a variety of Marjoram	Typical Mediterranean flavour.	Used in conjunction with pasta, rice & tomato dishes.
PARSLEY	Found everywhere, leaves are shiny dark green, being finely divided.	Fresh & pleasant flavour.	Highest in vitamins. Can be used in abundance, very versatile.
ROSEMARY	An evergreen shrub, originally from Mediterranean. Has many branches with leathery, almost spiky thick green leaves.	Pungent, slight, pine flavour.	Good with casseroles, tomatoes, cauliflower & pulses.
SAGE	Is a shrubby plant with oblong leaves.	Strongest flavour of all the herbs not unlike camphor.	Good with cheese (Sage Derby) add to cream cheese, Welsh rarebit & pulse dishes.
TARRAGON	Green shrub found in dry climates, cultivated for its leaves. 2 types – French & Russian, latter has lesser flavour.	Has distinctive smell & taste.	Makes a lovely vinegar, good with green salads & egg dishes.
THYME	A small shrubby plant with a woody stem and small leaves. It has small bluish-purple leaves.	Spicy taste & odour.	Very versatile use as general flavouring.

4. *Spices*

For hundreds of years, trading in spices has been vital to the economic state of many tropical countries. Europeans have always been anxious to buy anything that would help preserve their food, especially meat, which was not always as fresh as it might have been. The addition of spices helped to improve what must have been a far from desirable taste.

Spice countries therefore wielded a great deal of power. Before too long, control was taken over by the East India Company and by 1600 the British East India Company had been formed, to look after her own interests in that part of the world, with the added bonus that spices became much cheaper in this country. The new found abundance of spices, all but swamped British cookery, not to mention the great interest that developed in the cuisine of these foreign countries. Recipes for chutneys and curries were sent home by travellers and soon became an important part of our way of life.

BUYING SPICES

1. Where possible, buy whole spices in a loose state then grind them when required.

2. Only buy in small quantities as they do eventually become stale tasting, regular replenishing will ensure they are as fresh as possible.

3. Packet spices have often been stored in the light and are quite often older than they should be. If this is the case, they will have lost their distinctive fresh flavour and smell.

4. Always buy your spices from a shop with a good stock turn over, so what you are purchasing will be as fresh as possible.

STORAGE

1. Spices should be stored in air-tight containers or screw top jars, in a cool dark place. If they are exposed to too much light, they lose their potency.

2. Store in small dark jars as found in kitchen shops. To minimise the air space (the flavours are volatile) keep the jars full whenever possible.

3. If you have a selection of spices on your kitchen wall, remove it!! These hot steamy conditions will do nothing for the flavour.

4. Although most whole spices will last for several years, that is no reason to keep them for that long! The maximum should only ideally be a couple of months.

5. *Other Flavourings*
1. SALT
Too much in the diet is potentially harmful, especially if the
product used is ordinary table salt or common salt. This is
almost pure sodium chloride, which could cause an imbalance
in the body if taken in quantity. It is therefore strongly advised
that you use only sea salt and in moderation.
2. VEGETABLE STOCK CUBES OR CONCENTRATE.
Available with or without salt, usually made from vegetable fat,
yeast, extract, lactose, hydrolised vegetable protein, sunflower
oil, spices and vegetables. These are a convenient standby for
emergencies, but true vegetable stock is very simple to make,
see recipe on page 169.
3. SOYA SAUCE
This has been used in China since the sixth century. Today,
there are many varieties on the market;
    Tamari – is a soya sauce which is naturally fermented and
made without the use of chemicals.
    Soya sauce – is made from a mixture of wheat and soya beans,
soaked until soft, then cooked with water and sea salt. A
bacteria called 'Koji' is then added which enables fermentation
to take place. Pressing then takes place, and the resulting liquid
is heated to halt fermentation and preserve the flavour.
4. CAROB
Carob beans are the fruit of the carob tree which is grown in
warm climates. They are dark brown in colour, not unlike
runner beans to look at. When these are ripe, the pods are
crushed, the pulpy portion of the bean is then separated from
the hard seed. This is ground to a fine powder which can be
made into chocolate bars or powder for eating or use in baking.
It is a far better product than chocolate, it is rich in vitamins and
minerals, contains no refined sugar or habit forming caffeine
and produces no more guilty feelings!!

TABLE OF SPICES – 1

SPICE	APPEARANCE	FLAVOUR	USES
ALLSPICE	Dried berry of the evergreen Myrtle family. Black/brown colour, slightly bigger than a black peppercorn, with smooth skin.	Described as a combination of Cloves, Cinnamon & Nutmeg, hence the name Allspice.	Pickles, marinades, curries, sweet & savoury dishes. Add a few to your pepper mill.
CARAWAY	Small brown crescent-shaped seed.	Distinctive spicy taste.	Use with cream cheese, cabbage, cheese biscuits, goulash. Decoration for bread.
CARDAMON SEEDS	Sold in the pod. Expensive because they are hand picked.	Strong flavour	Used in lentil dishes, curries & milk puddings.
CAYENNE PEPPER	Reddish in colour, can only be bought ground, therefore buy in small quantities.	Hot & peppery	Use sparingly on egg and cheese dishes.
CHILLI	Sold whole & in powdered form. WHOLE: Small pointed pepper bought fresh or dried. Pungency can be reduced by removing seeds. POWDER: Ground dried Chilli peppers.	Hot and firey.	Mexican dishes.

TABLE OF SPICES – 2

SPICE	APPEARANCE	FLAVOUR	USES
CINNAMON	Comes from the bark of a tree from the Laurel family. Sold as quills – finely rolled bark or as powder. It is difficult to grind at home so use powdered form for cakes, biscuits.	Spicy wood smell, unmistakable flavour	POWDER: Cakes, biscuits, mincemeat & savoury dishes. QUILLS: flavours milk & cream for puddings & sauces, poached fruit.
CLOVES	Dried flower buds of evergreen tree from Myrtle family. Bought whole or powdered, difficult to grind yourself.	Pungent.	WHOLE: pickling, stick into fruit or onion for flavour. Gives apple pie special taste. POWDERED: Christmas cake & pudding, yeast items, mulled wine.
CORIANDER	Round pale coloured seeds. Always buy whole if possible, easily crushed at home. Sold in powdered form, fawn coloured in this state.	Subtle smell & flavour.	Curry, vegetable dishes, pulses.
CUMIN	Light brown powder & seeds.	Pungent flavour	Vital in Middle Eastern dishes. Seeds should be heated in pan before use to bring out flavour. Beautiful distinctive addition to vegetable dishes.

TABLE OF SPICES – 3

SPICE	APPEARANCE	FLAVOUR	USES
CURRY POWDER	Curry powder is a combination of many different spices, it is very easy to make yourself. You will notice the difference – commercial curry powder is a harsh comparison.	With homemade curry it is possible to distinguish the different flavours nutmeg, cardamon, cloves, cumin, chilli, cinnamon & mace. Colour will depend on quantities of the above.	Used in curry dishes, good with egg & cheese dishes, can be added to mayonnaise.
GINGER	It is an aromatic knotty root, thick & fibrous in appearance either white or buff-coloured. Ground ginger is light brown.	Easily recognisable.	Curry, biscuits & cakes, flavouring oil in frying. Crystallisd ginger & stem ginger for baking.
JUNIPER BERRIES	They are blue-black berries	Tastes like gin.	Used to stimulate appetite. Used in the production of gin, for stocks, pies and casseroles.
MACE	Outer covering of nutmeg. Sold in blades – little sharp pieces or ground.	Stronger than nutmeg.	BLADES: used in milk sauce infusions. POWDERED: savoury dishes, mincemeat.
MIXED SPICE	Light nutty brown.	Is a mixture of Cloves, Cinnamon, Nutmeg & Allspice.	Cakes, biscuits, puddings & sweet yeast doughs.
MUSTARD	Basic form is white or black mustard seed, they are hottest in the whole form. Seeds are ground to make powdered mustard.	Hot & spicy.	Enhances cheese dishes & sauces, dressing & mayonnaise. Use as general flavouring.

TABLE OF SPICES – 4

SPICE	APPEARANCE	FLAVOUR	USES
NUTMEG	Whole nut is about ½" long & nutty brown in colour, it is the best way to use it, grating it as required. It is sold in powdered form.	Perfumed & nutty.	Add to cooked vegetables, sauces, cheese dishes & milk puddings.
PAPRIKA	It is the ground seeds of the sweet pepper. Comes in mild & sweet form, always sold in powdered form.	Quite hot & spicy.	Adds piquancy to cheese dishes, good for decorating.
PEPPERCORNS	GREEN PEPPERCORNS: are unripe peppercorns, sold pickled in brine.	Green: Hot & firey, rinse away the brine.	Green, use as for capers in sauces & as decoration.
	WHITE PEPPERCORNS: less common in their whole state, have harsher taste & are less aromatic than	White: harsh almost bitter taste.	Use pepper as general seasoning.
	BLACK PEPPERCORNS: small black & shrivelled looking.	Black: smooth aromatic flavour.	
POPPY SEEDS	Tiny black balls.	Nutty flavour.	Used as decoration on breads or cheese biscuits.
TURMERIC	Bright yellow & sold already ground, it comes from the root of a plant related to ginger.	Strong flavour.	Used in Indian dishes, can replace saffron for colour, use sparingly as it is strong.

Thick Homemade Tomato Sauce

1 large onion – peeled, roughly chopped
oil
1 clove garlic – peeled, crushed
15 oz *(425 g)* tinned tomatoes
3 tablespoons tomato purée
1 bay leaf
1 teaspoon oregano
1 teaspoon basil
1 teaspoon thyme
salt and freshly ground pepper

This is really quick and simple to make, it is very versatile so always keep some in the fridge.

1 Gently soften the onion and garlic in a saucepan in a little oil. Cook until the onion is transparent.

2 Once the onion is soft add all the other ingredients, simmer gently for 15–20 minutes until the sauce thickens.

3 Season with salt and pepper to taste.

Leave to cool. Store in an air-tight container in the fridge, use as required.

If you prefer a smoother texture, liquidise the sauce and remember to remove the bay leaf first!

Brown Onion Sauce

2 onions – peeled – either roughly chopped or sliced depending on the sort of finished texture you require
1 oz *(25 g)* butter or margarine
1 oz *(25 g)* wholewheat flour
½ pt – ¾ pt *(275–425 ml)* good vegetable stock
1 teaspoon yeast extract
Worcester sauce
salt and pepper

1 Soften the onion in the fat, cook over a moderate heat until the fat begins to brown and colour the onion. Try to achieve a deep nut brown colour without burning.

2 Add the flour, stir well and cook for a few minutes.

3 Remove from the heat, gradually add the vegetable stock, stir well, add the yeast extract, bring to the boil, reduce to a simmer until the desired thickness of sauce is obtained.

Season with the salt and freshly ground pepper and Worcester sauce to taste.

Mayon-naise

2 egg yolks
1 teaspoon mustard
½ pt *(275 ml)* oil (or ¼ pt *(150 ml)* of olive and salad oil for example)
a squeeze of lemon juice
1 tablespoon white wine vinegar
salt and pepper

1 Beat the yolks and the mustard together in a bowl with either an electric or hand whisk.

2 Add the oil to the yolks a drop at a time, whisking well in between each addition. This is very important as it is in these early stages that curdling is liable to occur.

3 Keep the oil coming slowly, if the mayonnaise begins to thicken and is smooth in texture it will be alright. Stop after half the oil has been used. Beat in the lemon juice, then continue with the rest of the oil, you can pour a little quicker now.

4 Still whisking, dribble in the vinegar, then add the salt and pepper to taste.

If the mixture does curdle – that is, it looks thin and separates into two layers, with the oil on the top and egg on the bottom, stop! It is possible to save it if you have not gone too far, so stop adding the oil as soon as it happens.

Separate another egg, put the yolk into a clean bowl. Beat in the curdled mixture drop by drop, whisk all the time. Once the curdled mixture is incorporated, continue as above.

Mayonnaise can be made in a liquidiser or food processor. The temptation is to add the oil too quickly, so it would be a good idea to make it by hand a couple of times to serve as a reminder of just how careful you must be.

Basic White Sauce

1 oz *(25 g)* butter or margarine
1 oz *(25 g)* wholewheat flour
½ pt *(275 ml)* milk, infuse with slices of onion, carrot, celery, bay leaf and mixed herbs (optional)

1 For a sauce full of flavour, gently heat the milk with the vegetables for about 7–10 minutes.

2 Melt the fat in another saucepan, add the flour, mix well and cook for a minute, this is called the roux.

3 Take the saucepan off the heat and gradually add the milk (through a sieve if it has been infusing, the vegetables are no longer needed) stir well to make a smooth sauce. If you should get lumps, use a small hand whisk and beat quickly.

4 Return to the heat, stir until it boils and thickens. Season with salt and freshly ground pepper. Use as required.

Two Homemade Curry Powders

A. Makes 2 oz *(50 g)*

¼ oz *(7 g)* ground cloves
¾ oz *(20 g)* cardamon seeds
¼ oz *(7 g)* ground cumin
½ teaspoon of chilli powder
¾ oz *(20 g)* ground cinnamon
1 whole nutmeg – grated
1 pinch of ground mace

B. Makes enough for one curry

2 teaspoons turmeric
½ teaspoon ground ginger
1 clove of garlic – crushed
1½ teaspoons ground coriander
¼ teaspoon salt
¼ teaspoon cayenne

Put all the ingredients together in a bowl and mix. Store A in an airtight jar, use B straight away.

Easy Mixed Herb Oil

1 pt *(575 ml)* **sunflower oil**
a small bunch of parsley – chopped
2 teaspoons dried thyme
2 teaspoons dried marjoram

Combine all the ingredients in a jar with a good screw top. Leave to stand in the fridge for 8–10 days. It will need a regular shake. Give the oil a good shake before use. The herbs need to be covered in oil at all times so keep the jar topped up.

Single Fresh Herb Oil

¾ pt *(425 ml)* **sunflower or olive oil**
2–3 sprigs of fresh herbs eg.
    rosemary, thyme, basil or sage

Put the chosen herb and the oil into a screw top jar. Leave to stand for 1–2 weeks. Give the jar a regular shake.

Do not keep oils like this for more than 6 weeks as they begin to look a bit stale as the herb gets older.

Lemon Vinegar

½ pt *(275 ml)* **white wine vinegar**
1 lemon – juice and zest

Thinly peel the skin off the lemon taking care not to include the white pith, this is the bitter bit.
Squeeze the lemon.

Combine all the ingredients in a screw top jar. Leave in the fridge to stand for 3 weeks.

When ready to use, strain the vinegar to remove the lemon. Return the vinegar to the jar.

Garlic Vinegar

6 cloves garlic – peeled, crushed
1 sprig of thyme (or ½ teaspoon of dried)
1 teaspoon white peppercorns
¾ pt *(425 ml)* red wine vinegar

Wash and dry the fresh thyme, (put the dried thyme straight into the jar) put into the jar with the vinegar and the peeled garlic. Screw on the top and store for three weeks in the fridge. Shake regularly. When ready to use, strain off the garlic and herbs, return to the jar.

Burger Relish

Mix together:
½ red pepper – washed, deseeded, finely chopped
½ green pepper – washed, deseeded, finely chopped
¼ onion – peeled, finely chopped or spring onions – finely sliced
6 oz *(175 g)* cooked sweetcorn
1 tablespoon parsley – finely chopped
2 good teaspoons French or German mustard
¼ pt *(150 ml)* mayonnaise

Season with salt and freshly ground pepper.

Basic Vegetable Stock

2 medium onions – cut in half, not peeled

2 medium carrots – washed, broken in half

2 sticks celery – washed, broken in half

1 small leek – washed, roughly sliced

2 bay leaves

2 teaspoons mixed herbs

black peppercorns – crushed

} Bouquet garni

Well flavoured stock is the basis of all good soups, sauces, stews and casseroles.

Vegetable stock is the easiest and quickest to make as there is practically no preparation.

1 Half fill your largest possible saucepan (approx 12 pints/7 litres) with vegetable bits. Adjust the quantities above to fit your pan and for your own requirements.

2 Pour enough water to come within 2" (6 cm) of the top. If you have any left-over vegetable water or white bean cooking liquid add this and make up the difference with plain water. The brown bean water is inclined to be a bit on the bitter side so adding this might affect the more delicate things you might want to use the stock for.

3 2 tablespoons of Tamari sauce (soy) can be added to increase the protein level of the stock.

4 Cover the pan and bring to the boil, reduce the heat to a simmer, cook for about 2 hours to extract as much flavour from the vegetables as possible. Cool the stock.

5 Strain the cooled liquid through a sieve to catch all the bits.

6 Store in a sealed container near the top of the fridge where it will keep for a week or more.

As you can see, it is extremely quick to make and well worth it for the wonderful smell and the added depth of taste it will give your cooking, not to mention the satisfaction of knowing *nothing* goes to waste in the kitchen!

It is a good idea to keep a bag of vegetable trimmings in the fridge. Start collecting a couple of days before you intend to make stock. Include things like: Pepper tops, Trimmings from root vegetables, Cauliflower/spinach/spring green/cabbage stalks and outer leaves, Runner bean trimmings, Pea and bean pods.

I do not use tomatoes or potatoes as I think they make a bitty end result.

Fresh Fruit Sauce

1 lb fresh fruit eg. apples, blackcurrants, raspberries, blackberries or cranberries
3 tablespoons water
Sugar or honey to taste

1 Place the desired fruit into a saucepan with the water. Cover and cook very slowly until the fruit is soft.

2 Using a sieve and wooden spoon, sieve the fruit into a bowl. The sieve will catch the pips and bits of tough skin. If you prefer to keep the skin in the final sauce as in the case of apple sauce, just core the apples before cooking.

3 Add sugar or honey to taste if required.

Apple sauce can be made with the addition of the zest of a lemon, add a knob of butter for a richer tasting sauce.

Cranberry sauce is delicious with the zest and juice of an orange, no water is needed.

Combination sauces can be made eg. raspberry and strawberry sauce, blackcurrant and damson sauce.

Sweet White Sauce

½ pt (275 ml) milk
1 vanilla pod
1 tablespoon cornflour
1 tablespoon golden granulated sugar

1 In a saucepan, warm the milk with the vanilla pod.
2 In a bowl combine the cornflour and the sugar with a little of the warming milk.
3 When the milk comes up to the boil, remove the pod and combine the milk gradually with the flour and sugar, return to the heat to thicken.

Serve and use as custard.

The slower the milk comes to the boil in the first stage the more likely it is to have a good vanilla flavour.

Wash the vanilla pod, dry well and use again.

Vinaigrette

3 tablespoons of good oil
1 tablespoon white wine vinegar (or cider vinegar or red wine vinegar)
salt and freshly ground pepper
a pinch of mustard powder (½ teaspoon made mustard)
a pinch of sugar (optional)
1 squeeze of lemon

Also known as French Dressing.

Put all the ingredients together into a screw top jar and shake or whisk thoroughly in a small bowl.

This basic dressing can be flavoured with chopped herbs, crushed garlic, mint sauce concentrate, orange juice (and zest for extra bite) not to mention using flavoured oils and vinegars.

Sweeteners

No sugar is really very good for us. It is a well known contributing factor to tooth decay, not to mention the extra calories sweet goods contain. Some types are however slightly better than others so do search out and experiment with the unrefined alternatives – these varieties are far superior in flavour and nutritional value, and lower in calories.

NATURAL SOURCES OF SWEETNESS

1. HONEY

Honey is a sweet, sticky, golden yellow liquid made by bees. They collect the nectar from the flowers which is then processed by enzymes in their stomachs. These substances start converting the sugar in the nectar. This liquid is then deposited and stored in hexagonal wax compartments in which the conversion of the sugar continues. The wax cells are made into blocks or combs which gradually become filled with honey as we know it.

The flavour of the final honey will depend on the type of flowers the bees have visited, often giving distinctive tastes and smells, e.g. Heather honey is dark in colour with a strong flavour. This aspect makes each honey a very individual product. The single nectar honey will be expensive, which is why the cheaper varieties contain a mixture from various honey producing countries. This makes more sense for everyday use, especially if it is to be used for cooking.

Honey comes in clear or cloudy forms. The clear honey has been heat treated to stop it from clouding, which is something that will happen to all honey eventually. This type is good for cooking as it dissolves quickly. Cloudy honey tastes more sugary, often having crystals in it. Nutritionally, honey contains small amounts of B vitamins like B_2 and niacin with traces of a wide selection of minerals. It contains sugar in the form of fructose or fruit sugar, which is supposed to be better for you than sucrose. Honey is low in calories and provides a good source of energy that is quickly available to the body.

Storage
Honey must be kept in a warm place, otherwise it will start to crystallise. If this does happen, it can easily be rectified by placing the jar in some hot water.

Cooking with honey
1. When baking with honey, use a light coloured one otherwise it tends to make the finished article look a little on the dark side.
2. Do not use one with a very distinctive flavour unless this is going to be a feature of the dish – honey imparts a definite taste anyway.
3. 10 ounces (300 g) of sugar should be replaced by ½ pound (225 g) of honey – use as a guideline for recipe alterations. REMEMBER to reduce the amount of liquid by 3 tablespoons for this amount.

2. MAPLE SYRUP

Maple syrup comes from the maple tree that grows in Canada. It has a bitter-sweet taste, not unlike caramel toffee – which makes its uses fairly limited. Traditionally, it is used on waffles and with ice-cream or how about as a sauce for a sponge pudding?

The best quality is fairly light in colour and, once opened, it should be stored in the fridge, otherwise mould might appear. Crystallisation could occur, but it is easily solved by putting the jar in some hot water.

It is an expensive product, but well worth it once in a while.

3. NATURAL SUGARS

There is no real reason why we should add extra sugar to our food, because in actual fact, there is plenty that occurs naturally in primary foods – milk, fruit and vegetables. These contain the natural sugars – Lactose, Glucose and Fructose. Having said that, most people are introduced to extra sugar at an early age which gives them a sweet tooth, things then just do not taste the same without it. If you glance at the labels on processed foods, it is surprising how many of them have sugar high on their list of ingredients, another reason to steer well clear of them.

SUGAR

Sugar in the form most familiar to everyone is the sweetness contained in the ripening sap of the sugar cane or sugar beet plant. This is in a concentrated form and thanks to modern technology, it can be extracted economically and refined to a variety of stages. Each product has distinctive characteristics. In its unrefined state, sugar contains fibre, vitamins and minerals including iron, potassium, calcium and a certain percentage of water. White sugar at the other end of the cycle consists of more or less pure glucose, no fibre, vitamins or minerals, and therefore should be avoided.

The Properties of Sugar
Sugar, be it refined, unrefined, natural or chemically reproduced has extraordinary qualities. Many preparations, whether we agree with them or not, would not exist without it, e.g. baking, canning, bottling and preserving.
1. It does not decompose or smell when heated and can be dissolved with or without the use of a liquid as in the case of caramel. Here, sugar is gradually heated until it dissolves, the increasing temperature eventually turns the sugar into the dark, sticky, liquid caramel.
2. It adds bulk, e.g. whisking eggs and sugar together makes a thick mousse with a creamy texture.
3. It can be used to enhance flavours without necessarily adding sweetness, as in the case of adding a *pinch* to peas or tomatoes to bring out their natural sweetness, it acts in a similar way to salt.
4. Sugar acts as a food for yeast which is after all a living organism and so needs food, moisture and warmth to make it grow.
5. When egg whites are whisked, they contain a great deal of air. Sugar is added to the mixture to strengthen the structures formed, these will then be able to trap more air enabling the meringue to be whisked until firm peaks are formed.
6. Sugar is important in cake making as it combines with the fat during creaming or beating and traps air. This allows the gluten

in the flour to retain a soft structure enabling the cake to rise.

7. Sugar keeps the product fresh tasting as it retains moisture and helps to control the final texture of the cake or biscuit.

8. Sugar acts as a preservative in jams, marmalades, fruit cheeses and jellies.

Substituting Unrefined Sweeteners for White Sugar
You do not have to treat cooking with brown sugar any differently: cream, rub in or melt the sugar with the fat according to the recipe in just the same way. The only difference is, you will have a far wider choice of sweeteners as there a great variety of tastes and textures which will add new interest to your cooking.

a) Use the full amount of just one of the unrefined sugars according to the recipe.

b) Use half one sort of sugar and half another e.g. Barbados and Golden granulated in flapjack for a less toffee-like final result.

c) Use ¾ the recipe's amount of sugar making the remainder up with Molasses syrup, this would be excellent in a sticky gingerbread.

d) Use ¾ the sugar requirement in honey alone, remembering to remove 3 tablespoons of liquid from the recipe.

TYPES OF SUGAR
Demerara
Is so called because it comes from Demerara in Guyana. It has large brown crystals containing a small amount of vitamins and minerals. BEWARE there is a Demerara sugar available that is just coloured white sugar so check the label. If the packet states the country of origin it is a genuine product. This applies to all types of sugar.

Golden granulated
This is a fairly new product and is a natural unrefined cane sugar produced in Mauritius. It replaces ordinary white refined granulated sugar in all uses, in cooking, tea and coffee. If you want a light sponge or a more delicate flavour, this is the sugar to use.

Barbados (Muscovado)
Is a soft dark brown sugar that comes from the bottom of the refining pan. It has more vitamins and minerals than Demerara and can be used for all types of cooking, giving the final product a dark colour with a very moist texture. It is therefore ideal for breads and cakes.

Molasses sugar
This is the richest of all the sugars as far as vitamins and minerals are concerned, being really dark in colour and tasting very much like treacle toffee. It is excellent for items like ginger fruit cakes and tea breads. It will be too rich tasting for lighter items.

Raw sugar
Is dark brown and has large crystals and sometimes includes a large proportion of molasses.

DO NOT confuse these sugars with those termed soft brown which are refined sugars often described as being similar in texture to damp sand! The colour varies from light beige to dark brown with a variety of different tastes too.

SUGAR BY-PRODUCTS
During sugar refining, several syrups are extracted from the process and sold commercially.

Black Strap Molasses
This is at the opposite end to white sugar in the processing cycle. It only contains ⅔rds of the calories of white sugar with a trace of protein and a number of different vitamins and minerals. It is thick and dark in appearance with a strong flavour so use it with care. Probably its best use is in conjunction with an unrefined sugar in things like tea bread and gingerbread.

Black Treacle
Is obtained from the early stages of sugar refining. It is a thick sticky substance with a distinctive strong flavour, and is not as overpowering as molasses.

Golden Syrup
This is a partially inverted sugar syrup which means it has partially been divided into two constituents, glucose and fructose. It is sweeter and more refined than the others.

Beginners Guide to Bread Making

There is without doubt, nothing that compares with the smell of freshly baked bread. Making your own bread each week really is an enjoyable exercise and rather relaxing, especially when you know the finished loaf will be of far superior quality and taste to anything you will be able to buy in the shops.

Bread making is an art. Yeast is not always the easiest organism to work with, but once you understand how the different ingredients work, and react together, it will make things a great deal simpler.

All you will need is: strong wholewheat flour, yeast, liquid at blood temperature, a pinch of salt, a knob of fat for flavour and a little of something sweet.

STRONG FLOUR

You will only be able to make a good loaf of bread in both taste and size from a strong flour which is a mixture of 'hard' grained American or Canadian wheat and the 'soft' grained English wheat. Bread flour or strong flour contains Gluten.

Gluten is the most important element in the bread flour. It is activated when warm liquid is added. This causes the protein stored in the starch grains to break out. The resulting reaction produces an elastic dough. Gluten forms the structure of the loaf, that is, strands that will collect air, and gently expand to form a wall of air bubbles – these give the bread a good finished height.

Once the dough is put in the oven, these air-filled gluten structures harden and set to form a firm loaf in the familiar shape. Gluten is strengthened by the addition of salt. Should you forget it, the dough will be sticky and difficult to handle, and lacking in taste. The gluten is also strengthened and the texture improved by a process called kneading. This makes the dough more elastic and ensures a good rise.

It is always worth checking a particular brand of flour, to see if it is suitable for bread making.

KNEADING

This is the movement of the dough using the palm of the hand and the knuckles, whereby the dough is stretched and pushed.
1. Put the dough on a lightly floured surface. Stretch half of the dough, the half furthest away, using the palm of your hand.
2. Grab hold of the end you have just pushed away, lift it up and punch it back into the main lump of the dough.
3. Turn the dough, repeat the process until the texture is smooth and no longer sticks.
   This is the therapeutic bit!

YEAST

Yeast is a rising agent. It comes in two forms, fresh and dried which must not be confused with Brewers yeast which comes in powdered or tablet form.

Yeast is a living organism and so requires moisture (water or milk), food (sugar/honey/malt/molasses) and warmth (a warm atmosphere) in order to grow. As it does so, it gives off carbon dioxide which helps the dough to rise. As the gas expands, the elastic cell walls of the gluten stretch to form a risen structure.

FRESH YEAST is available from health food shops and some supermarkets. It is a light putty colour with a smooth texture and a delicate yeasty smell. It is a perishable product so it is essential that it is 100% fresh when purchased. It should therefore be creamy to putty in colour without any sign of browning around the edges (a sign of drying out), it should be cool to the touch and when crumbled it should break easily with only a slight smell of yeast.

AVOID yeast that is streaked with brown or dark yellow, sticky to touch or that smells unpleasant.

STORAGE

Wrapped in foil yeast can be kept in the fridge for 4 days. Wrapped in foil in the ice compartment of the fridge it will keep for up to 4 months. Wrapped in 1 ounce (25 g) bits it can be frozen for up to a year – this makes buying fresh yeast more convenient as you can buy a block and divide it up.

DRIED YEAST is more readily available from chemists, supermarkets, health shops and very often local shops, this is because it has been dehydrated and so is easier to store. It has the same properties as fresh yeast but has to be reactivated before use. As it is more potent, you will only need half the weight specified for a fresh yeast recipe.

Method

Add yeast to at least four times its own weight of warm liquid as given in the recipe, with a teaspoon of something sweet to act as a food. This is left in a warm place to multiply and becomes very frothy looking.

When using yeast it is important to have all the ingredients and equipment warm: warm liquid, warm flour, warm bowls etc, as a sharp change in temperature, be it hot or cold, could kill the yeast. For the same reason, warm the bread tins before you put the bread dough in to rise for the second time, this makes the final proving stage quicker.

Quick acting yeast (easy blend): This is the type of yeast that might well get you into the habit of making bread. It is good for beginners as it cuts out stage two.

All you have to do is combine all the dry ingredients (no sugar is required) including the yeast, then add the warm liquid, mix with a spoon to combine everything. Knead, then continue as for the other methods.

Basic Whole-wheat Bread

1 oz *(25 g)* fresh yeast (if using dried yeast or 'Easy blend' yeast refer to instructions on packet)
1 teaspoon of Barbados sugar
½ pt *(275 ml)* warm water
1 lb *(450 g)* strong wholewheat flour
1 teaspoon salt

1 Put the flour and salt into a warm bowl, leave in a warm place.

2 a) Crumble the fresh yeast into a bowl, mix with the sugar, then add half the liquid. Leave somewhere warm to ferment, use within 5 minutes.

b) For the dried yeast, dissolve the sugar in half the warm liquid, sprinkle the yeast on the top, leave in a warm place for 10 minutes.

3 When the yeast has 'sponged' (become active and frothy) add to the flour with the remaining liquid and mix. The 'Easy blend' method begins here.

4 Once the flour is incorporated, the dough is turned out of the bowl onto a lightly floured surface and kneaded until it becomes smooth and elastic. The time will depend on your technique; anything from 7–10 minutes.

5 Put the dough to rise in a clean, dry, large, warm bowl, cover with a damp cloth or put in a plastic bag and leave in a warm place for about an hour until it doubles in size. Grease a 2 lb or two 1 lb bread tins, put somewhere warm.

6 Once risen, the dough must be knocked back. Here the air is punched out as it is kneaded back to its original size. At this stage, it can be shaped into buns, rounds, plaits, cottage loaves or put straight into the warmed tin(s). Cover with a dry cloth or put back in the plastic bag and place in a warm place. This stage is called proving and takes about 20 minutes depending on the heat.

7 Once the loaf has proved; that is doubled again in bulk, and looks a good shape and size – the dough should come ½" above the edge of the tin – cook in a preheated oven.

8 The dough will continue to rise further once in the oven, but when the temperature reaches 60°c (140°f) the yeast is killed. Cook until the loaf sounds hollow when tapped on the bottom of the tin. Using a cloth, turn the bread out; if the bottom and sides still look a little pale, put it back in the oven, bottom side up for a few more minutes.

9 Cool bread out of its tin on a wire rack to allow the steam to escape, thus lightening the bread still further. After 2 hours, the bread will slice quite easily. Wait until the bread is stone cold before putting it away. If stored warm it will go soggy or even mouldy.
Use proper bread tins if you can, they are inexpensive and come in one or two pound tins, grease them before use each time but never wash them once they have been used.

Bibliography

I found these books very interesting reading:

Diet for a small plant: Frances Moore Lappé, Ballantine Books, New York, 1975

The Wholefood Cookbook: Gail Duff, Marshall Cavendish, 1980

Vegetarian Cookbook: Gail Duff, Pan Books, 1978

Vegetables: The Good Cook, Time Life Books, 1978

The Herb Book: John Lust, Bantam Books, 1974

Good Cooking: Marshall Cavendish, 1976–1977

The Fruit and Nut Book: Helena Radecka, Phoebe Phillips Editions, 1984

Useful Addresses

The Vegetarian Society of the UK Ltd, Parkdale, Dunham Road, Altrincham, Cheshire WA14 4QG (London Office: 53 Marloes Road, London W8 6LA)

The Vegan Society Ltd, 33–35 George Street, Oxford

Index